The Spiritual Art of Being Organized

by

CLAIRE JOSEFINE

Winter's Daughter Press

The Spiritual Art of Being Organized

by Claire Josefine

Winter's Daughter Press

Eureka, CA 95503

organized@humboldt1.com

www.clairejosefine.com

1-800-505-3881

0 9 8 7 6 5 4 3 2 1

Library of Congress Cataloging in Publication Data

Josefine, Claire.

The Spiritual Art of Being Organized/Claire Josefine

Includes bibliography and index.

ISBN 0-9747372-4-0

1. Organization. 2. Simplicity. 3. Spirituality. 4. Conduct of Life. 5. Quality of Life. 6. Stress Management. 7. Time Management. 8. Home Economics.

Library of Congress Control Number 2004103282

Printed in the United States of America

Notice of Liability: This publication contains the opinions and ideas of the author. It is intended to provide helpful and informative material on the subject matter covered. It is sold with the understanding that the author and publisher are not engaged in rendering professional services in the book. If the reader requires personal assistance or advice, a competent professional should be consulted. The author and publisher specifically disclaim any responsibility for any liability, loss, or risk, personal or otherwise, that is incurred as a consequence, directly or indirectly, of the use and application of any of the contents of this book.

The following authors and publishers have graciously granted permission to include the following:

"Repair of the World" by Naomi Newman. Copyright © 1994 by Naomi Newman, 80 Rowan Way, Mill Valley, CA 94941 (email: naomizn@rcn.com).

"The Red Wheelbarrow" by William Carlos Williams, from *Collected Poems: 1909-1939, Volume 1,* Copyright © 1938 by New Directions Publishing Corp. Reprinted by permission of New Directions Publishing Corp.

"The Peace of Wild Things" from *Collected Poems: 1957-1982* by Wendell Berry. Copyright © 1985 by Wendell Berry. Reprinted by permission of North Point Press, a division of Farrar, Straus and Giroux, LLC.

"Satori" by Carla Baku. Copyright © 2002 by Carla Baku.

"Ten Universal Laws of the Warrior Code" by Dawn Callan. Copyright © 1995 by Dawn Callan.

Dedicated to my parents

Table of Contents

Introduction

Give up on yourself. Begin taking action now, while being neurotic or imperfect, or a procrastinator or unhealthy or lazy or any other label by which you inaccurately describe yourself. Go ahead and be the best imperfect person you can be and get started on those things you want to accomplish before you die.

— Shoma Morita

Being organized is a spiritual process. Chaos is conquered as much by awareness, gratitude, grounding, and breath as by a well-labeled filing system.

Most books cover the external aspects of organizing, teaching us various tricks of the trade. But these tricks are only half the solution. Unless we make the internal changes necessary to maintain our newly found organization, unless we change how we move through our world, we relapse into chaos. It is not enough to set up organizing systems; we must modify our behavior and beliefs so that we can use those systems effectively. We must become more aware of our actions, slow down, and adopt an attitude of gratitude—realize that our lives are abundant with blessings, our needs met.

Not that this abundance is immediately apparent. We live in a crazy, fast-paced world, disconnected from our values and from each other; in a world driven by individualism and greed; a world of consumption and excess. Unless we make a conscious effort otherwise, our lives become a complicated juggling act of multiple jobs, appointments, housework, kids' activities, paper-work, deadlines—busyness magnified. This complex, busy world fosters disorganization, but doesn't require it. Simplicity and order are valid—even crucial—choices. And they are found within.

Before I Go Much Further

Allow me to introduce myself and this book. Have you ever looked up your name in one of those "what to name your baby" books? I did, and it turns out that my name means, roughly, "Giver of Light." I'm sure my parents had no idea of this when they gave the name to me, but it has proven to be an apt appellation.

Since 1996, my official title has been "professional organizer," which means that I help people eliminate clutter and implement simple organizational systems to make their lives easier. But I am really a teacher. My purpose is to learn, and then to share what I learn in order to make the world a bit more lovely and whole. And over the years I have learned much. I have worked as an office manager and bookkeeper for a variety of businesses, studied flower design, taught elementary school, tutored writing, worked as an editor and publishing consultant, dabbled in feng shui. I have also spent many years soaking up the spiritual lessons that relationships and healing have offered.

I believe that each step we take in life leads to the next, and that it is only by looking back that we can see how they form a clear (if winding) path. Each of my experiences has brought wisdom and skill to my role as an organizer. Now my experience as an organizer brings you this book. In it are gathered all the insights and lessons I have shared with clients and workshop students.

Here, then, is the light that I give you. Read it through, enjoy it, underline the parts that speak to you. Copy the 12 principles and post them on your refrigerator, or fold them into your wallet. Flip back and forth through the book, re-reading the sections that call to you. Different principles will apply at different times, in different circumstances. Learn them, even memorize them, let them become part of how you view the world. And then rest assured that, with these principles, you will be able to organize anything, anytime, anywhere, from now on.

Why Get Organized?

Why get organized? What are the benefits to you? When I ask my clients this question, they toss back answers:
♦ so I can find things;
♦ so I can pay my bills on time;
♦ so I can have company over without feeling embarrassed;
♦ to feel happier, more peaceful and serene;
♦ to reduce stress;
♦ to save time and effort, make my life easier;

- so I can meet deadlines, improving my work performance and relationships with co-workers;
- to save money (on late fees, duplication of possessions);
- to make money;
- to improve the way my home (or office) looks and feels;
- to have more time to spend with my family and to do what I really want;
- to feel better about myself.

Excellent reasons to become organized! And yet, some of us still resist. It helps to ask, "What would happen if I became organized?"

Sometimes, we use disorganization as protection. One woman I know felt that, as long as her home was in chaos, she couldn't have anyone visit. By repeatedly asking herself "what would happen if...? And then what would happen? And *then* what would happen?" she uncovered her underlying fear of rejection. She realized that she didn't want people to visit because she believed she was socially unacceptable, and keeping her home in chaos was her way of avoiding rejection.

Or there's the man with an overflowing garage. He believed that clearing the garage would force him to admit that his house had become too big now that the kids had grown and left. Admitting that the house was too big led to the conclusion that he'd have to move. Having to move brought forth that his marriage had been dead for some time. Hmmm... keep the garage cluttered and deny the marital problems, or clear the garage and face the relationship?

Some people resist becoming organized out of rebellion against authority or a fear of losing their creativity. People hang plaques in their homes proclaiming that "A clean home houses a dull woman." They equate organization and cleanliness with excessive control, repression, drudgery, and a lack of creativity. Yet often their disorganization prevents them from expressing their creativity! They can't find their materials or access their tools, or they spend so much time on other tasks that they have little time left for their art.

Artists, doctors, mothers, gardeners—I believe that each of us
has gifts to offer, and a duty to offer them. Each of us brings
something to the whole, to making the world a lovelier, safer,
happier place. Being organized helps us share our gifts.

What, then, does it mean to be organized? For me, being
organized means being able to access what we want quickly and easily. Organization does not require perfection, only that our systems are easy to use and maintain. Contrary to images of organized homes being the result of constant vigilance, organization is actually about being *lazy*; about making our lives easier. Rather than seeing organization as a dam that restricts our life's river, think of it as the raft that supports us, that provides structure and a modicum of safety and control as we float (or ride rapids) downstream.

> "If you feel constantly adrift but don't know why, be willing to explore the role that order—or the lack of it—plays in your life. No [one] can think clearly when constantly surrounded by clutter, chaos, and confusion, no matter who is responsible for it. Begin to think of order not as a straitjacket of "shoulds" (make the bed, wash the dishes, take out the garbage) but as a shape—the foundation—for the beautiful new life you are creating. It may be as simple as putting something back that you take out, hanging something up that you take off, or teaching those who live with you that they must do the same for the common good of all.
>
> There is a Divine Order—a Sublime Order—inherent in the Universe. We can tap into this powerful source of creative energy when we are willing to gradually cultivate a sense of order as to how we conduct our daily affairs. Invite Divine Order into your life today and a more serene tomorrow will unfold." *Sarah Ban Breathnach*

In fact, Class IV rapids are an excellent reason to become
organized. Life happens. We lose our job, our health, a loved
one. Or we become deeply involved in a creative project, a long

and fabulous vacation, an all-consuming love affair. We have babies, move, return to school, start a business, write a book, change careers. Being organized helps us to survive, even thrive, as we ride through these transitional rapids.

In *The Way of Zen*, Alan Watts wrote, "If the wind were to stop for one second for us to catch hold of it, it would cease to be wind. The same is true of life. Perpetually things and events are moving and changing…. We can only understand life by keeping pace with it, by a complete affirmation and acceptance of its magic-like transformations and unending changes." And, I would add, by being organized enough to flow with it.

So why get organized? Because, when all is said and done, being organized makes life easier.

The Juicy Stuff

As I was falling asleep one night, I was struck with a sudden realization: I needed to teach a class on organizing. Searching for a catchy title, I called the class "Zen and the Art of Being Organized." That class snowballed into a multitude of other classes, including classes on clutter clearing, paper management, kitchens, kids' rooms, surviving the holidays, and time management. At each class, I would write down organizing tools that the students already used, and then write down my list of organizing tips.

Frankly, after a while I tired of writing the same tips over and over. So I created a master list. Eventually, I edited this list, streamlining it into what I have identified as The 12 Basic Principles of Being Organized—both internal and external principles that I have since taught to hundreds of people. Just about any organizing tip you find anywhere is covered by these principles.

The purpose of this book is to share these 12 Basic Principles of Being Organized—practical and spiritual tools that reduce stress and increase joy. Interweaving Zen wisdoms, Hassidic tales, inspirational quotes, and poetry, I will elaborate upon each principle. But first, here they are *in toto*.

The 12 Basic Principles of Being Organized

1. Think! Think vertical, think verbs, think function, think consequences.
2. Put like with like within zones created by function.
3. K.I.S.S. (Keep It Simple, Sweetie).
4. Create, and use, habits and schedules.
5. Be realistic.
6. Set boundaries.
7. Dishes before dusting.
8. Slow down and pay attention.
9. Adopt an attitude of gratitude.
10. Base decisions in love instead of fear.
11. Remember that we have choices.
12. Ask for help.

1

Think!

A novice asked a master for instruction. The master replied, "Have you had your breakfast yet?" "I have," said the student. "Then wash your bowl," said the master.

When I was a teenager, my mother would inevitably get mad at me for some perceived idiocy. "Why didn't you *think*?" she'd scold. But how could I think of something if I hadn't thought of it? Without prior experience or modeling, the desired thoughts had no basis for existence.

Similarly, when I was studying for my elementary school teaching credential, I was introduced to the concept of "establishing schemata." Roughly, this is the process of introducing a framework for the information you are about to teach. If you want to teach kindergartners about elephants, you might ask the children if they've ever been to the zoo, what animals they've seen there, if they know anything about elephants. Then you might show them pictures of an elephant, or read them a story about elephants. Essentially what you are doing is giving them a context for the information you are about to impart, a container in which to file it. You are opening a file drawer and labeling a file for them in their brains.

Many disorganized people feel ashamed of their disorder, as though there were something wrong with them. Let me state emphatically: *Organizing is not a moral issue*. There is nothing fundamentally flawed in us if we are disorganized. More likely, we have never been taught how to organize: how to use space effectively, order objects, or look at the world with organized eyes. We have not been taught how to *think* organized. No one's ever set up an organizing file for us in our brains!

So, how should we think? We need to think vertically, think verbs, think function, and think consequences.

Think Vertical

We have a knack for sprawling horizontally, covering every desktop, table, counter, and dresser—sometimes every chair and floor, too! We make piles of paper, stacks of books; we spread our kitchen gadgets along our counters, our pocket change and earrings in a jumble on our dresser. Magazines and mail cover our coffee tables. Slightly worn clothes lie strewn across our bed or floor.

This tendency to spill over extends to our land-use practices, too. We build sprawling suburbs, covering prime agricultural land, pushing wildlife further into the margins until they have nowhere left to go, separating ourselves from each other, losing our center, our connections to community.

Sprawling doesn't work. Sane land-use calls for building up, not out. An organized home or office works on the same principle: up, not out. Use your walls and ceilings. Store books upright instead of in stacks. Put papers into containers that hold them upright—file, don't pile. Wherever and whenever you can, think vertical.

Here are some tools for vertical thinking.

1. **Use your walls.**
   ♦ Where can you put shelves? In addition to wall space, look for areas beneath counters and above windows and doors. You can even knock out the sheet rock on an internal wall and install shelves between two studs. Most closets have room for a second top shelf, too.
   ♦ Mount appliances on under-the-counter pull-out shelves to help declutter your kitchen counters.
   ♦ Screw in hooks to hold keys, coats, backpacks, and bags.
   ♦ Use wall clamps to hold brooms, mops, rakes, and shovels.
   ♦ Use pegboards and hooks or clamps to hold pots and pans, potholders, screwdrivers, wrenches, and hammers.
   ♦ Display jewelry on earring racks, or get creative and hang it on pieces of lace (for earrings), an attractive piece of driftwood with small nails hammered into it, or an expandable mug rack.
   ♦ Wall pockets are great for keeping paper separated by project, activity, or person.
   ♦ Install shelving units that fit over your toilet to add storage space for towels, soaps, toilet paper, or toiletries.

2. Use your ceilings.

♦ Hang 3-tiered baskets to store food, hand towels, hats and gloves, or other items.

♦ Pot racks free up cabinet space by storing pots and pans above your head where you can easily grab the ones you want. To avoid getting your pots grimy, do not hang the rack directly over your stove.

♦ Hang bicycles from ceiling hooks in your garage. Bicycle wall mounts are also available.

♦ Net hammocks work well for storing stuffed animals in kids' rooms. They can also be used for toys in the bathroom.

♦ Hooks for hanging plants allow you to enjoy indoor greenery without cluttering up counter space.

3. Use vertical containers.

♦ Magazine holders come in many styles, from cheap cardboard to fancy metal mesh. You can even make your own by cutting up a cereal box. And they can hold more than magazines. One busy government administrator had installed shelves, which she used for piles of written materials for her dozens of lectures and projects. By putting those piles upright into magazine holders, she liberated space on several shelves. And by labeling each magazine holder, she could readily identify each batch of paper. Magazine holders also prevented the papers from spilling over, making a mess, or getting lost.

♦ Tiered file holders allow you to wrangle desktop papers into clearly marked folders and store them upright while still being able to see them easily.

♦ Rolling units with stacked pull-out drawers are perfect for kids' rooms, offices, and artists' studios. Make life easier by labeling the contents of each drawer.

♦ Filing cabinets—and files—are a classic, efficient way to store and access paper. They are not at their best when used as catch-all drawers, however. I've seen more than one file drawer jumbled with computer hardware and stray manuals.

♦ Dressers seem to be my favorite furniture. I have a weakness for antique dressers, and use them throughout my home. I have drawers for clothes, obviously, but also for candles, table linens, canvas grocery bags, art supplies, photographs, and wrapping paper. And no, I do not have a junk drawer. Sorry!

I met a woman once, a sweet woman who collected cats. At the time I knew her, she had maybe two dozen cats in her small two-bedroom cottage. Her complaint was that the cats, in under-standable territorial manner, were peeing on every available surface. When I visited her home, I saw the problem. Other than in the kitchen, no horizontal surface was higher than three feet tall. Her mail (which she'd allowed to accumulate) was piled on a table by the front door, when it wasn't knocked to the floor or peed on by her cats. She had no bookshelves; even her bed was a mattress on the floor.

Being a cat-lover, I have occasional fantasies of being a cat-lady myself, but limit myself to a manageable five felines. That admitted, I still say this woman's problem wasn't really the cats. Her problem was a lack of vertical thinking. A couple of wall-pockets by the front door—one for incoming mail, the other for outgoing—work far better than a tabletop. Wall-mounted bookshelves at a height of five feet or higher would discourage cats from knocking over books and *tchotchkes* (knickknacks). A bed with pull-out drawers built into its frame would provide protected storage for bedding or clothes, as would a dresser.

Think Verbs

If you remember your grammar lessons, you'll recall that verbs are "action words." Every item that crosses our path requires some sort of action. Therefore, to organize our life, we need to think in terms of verbs. We need to ask, "What do I need to do with this thing, anyway? What action do I need to take?"

What kinds of actions are we likely to encounter? Let's run through some possible everyday verbs:

- ◆ clean
- ◆ repair
- ◆ toss
- ◆ put away
- ◆ pay
- ◆ fill out
- ◆ read
- ◆ write
- ◆ enter into computer
- ◆ file
- ◆ mail
- ◆ return
- ◆ call.

Clarifying the required action clears our disorganized muddle and helps us decide how to proceed. Instead of a daunting heap of unidentified items, we gain a series of specific tasks.

Think Function

In order to establish order, we ask and answer questions. We ask what has to happen with an item, and we ask how it's used. If we know how it's used, we know where to put it. After all, a single item has many potential uses, and therefore many possible homes.

For example, take a cast-iron skillet. Maybe I use it for cooking, in which case it lives in the kitchen. Maybe it's past its prime, but I want to use it as a planter for a succulent garden. (A vendor at my local farmers' market scavenges cast-off pots and pans and then plants beautiful succulent arrangements in them.) If the skillet is to be used for gardening, then it doesn't go in my kitchen; it goes with my gardening supplies. Or maybe I don't feel too green in the thumb, but am concerned about my safety. That cast-iron skillet makes a good *thunk;* if I'm using it for a weapon, maybe it lives by my bed!

By the way, the potential for multiple possible uses is why I organize my spices alphabetically. My father likes to group his by type: Italian together, baking together, and so on. But what about something like cinnamon, which can be used for baking, for Mexican, for Middle Eastern, and for East Indian? Rather than try to remember which use I was thinking of when I put the cinnamon away, I rely on the consistency of the alphabet. Cinnamon is always going to fall in the same place (between cayenne and cloves).

Think Consequences

Ah, here we have even more questions. What are the ramifications of our actions? Look at the whole picture.

◆ How much will this cost?
◆ Can I afford it?
◆ Where will I put it?
◆ What care will it require?
◆ What is the environmental impact?
◆ How will this affect my relationships?
◆ Do I even like it?

Thinking about consequences is particularly important when we are considering bringing yet another object, expense, or time commitment into our lives.

REPAIR OF THE WORLD
A *Kabbalistic creation story
© by Naomi Newman 1994

In the beginning,
before there were any beginnings or endings,
there was no place that was not already God.
We call this unimaginable openness
Ein Sof,
Being without end, world without end,
Ein Sof.
Then came the urge to give life
to our world and us.
But there was no place that was not already God.
So Ein Sof breathed in to make room
like a father steps back
so his child will walk to him.
We call this withdrawing
Tzim Tzum.

Into the emptiness Ein Sof set vessels
and began to fill them with divine light,
like a mother places bowls
in which to pour her delicious soup.
We call these bowls
Kaleem.

As the light poured forth a perfect world was
being created.
Think of it, a world without greed
and cruelty and violence.
But then something happened.
The kaleem shattered.
No one knows why.
Perhaps the bowls were too frail,
perhaps the light too intense,
perhaps Ein Sof was learning.
After all, no one makes perfect the first time.
With the shattering of the bowls
the divine sparks flew everywhere.
Some rushing back to Ein Sof,

some falling, falling,
trapped in the broken shards,
to become our world and us.

Though this is hard to believe,
the perfect world is all around us,
but broken into jagged pieces,
like a puzzle thrown to the floor,
the picture lost,
each piece without meaning
until someone puts them back together again.
We are that someone.
There is no one else.
We are the ones who can find the broken pieces,
remember how they fit together
and rejoin them.
And we call this repair of the world
Tikkun Olam.

In every moment with every act
we can heal our world and us.
We are all holy sparks dulled by separation.
But when we meet and talk and eat and make
love,
when we work and play and disagree
with holiness in our eyes,
seeing Ein Sof everywhere,
our brokenness will end.

Then our bowls will be strong enough to hold
the light,
and our light gentle enough to fill the bowls.
As we repair the world together,
we will learn
that there is no place
that is not
God.

This text is based on Rabbi Isaac Luria's (1534-1572) theory of
creation. After the expulsion of the Jews from Spain in 1492, Safed,
Palestine, became the center of a new form of Jewish mysticism.
Lurianic Kabbalah focused on the questions of suffering and evil and
how the world can be saved and redeemed.

2

Put Like with Like

within Zones

Created by Function

If a home doesn't make sense, nothing does.

— Henrietta Ripperge

I loved teaching elementary school math. The creativity possible was downright fun—and I say this as an English major! As much as I was teaching math, though, I was teaching my first-graders to think, to recognize patterns, sequences, and attributes.

Toward this end, we would play a game with Attribute Blocks, which were plastic cutouts in different shapes, sizes, and colors. We would take turns playing a block. Each block had to have at least one (or more, depending on how complex we made the game) attribute in common with the block before it. I might put down a large blue triangle, to which Susie would add a small blue circle, then Johnny would play a large green circle, and so on. We would continue playing, creating a snaking line of Attribute Blocks, each having something in common with its neighboring blocks.

Another game that the kids liked taught them to recognize attributes and to organize objects. (Believe it or not, children actually enjoy creating order.) I had assembled a junk box filled with a variety of objects: keys, coins, buttons, rocks, shells, feathers, empty wooden thread spools, erasers, whatever I could find. The game was simply to empty the box onto a table (or the floor), and then sort the items. There was no right or wrong answer; rather, the children created their own criteria for what went where.

I've also used this junk box game with adults to show them that they *do* know how to organize. It's especially fun with small groups of people. Each group determines its own criteria for sorting. When the sorting is done, they share which attributes they chose for sorting: color, size, texture, shape, function.

Zones

In her book, *Organizing from the Inside Out*, Julie Morgenstern introduces the concept of zones, using the kindergarten classroom as an example. Remember kindergarten? There was an area for playing with blocks, another for finger painting, another for naps, another for snacks, another for story-time. Each area had its requisite tools right there: blocks in the block zone; easels, paper, paint, and smocks in the painting zone; mats and blankets in the nap zone.

One of my clients playfully calls her zones "land." In her kitchen cupboards she has pasta land, soup land, baking land, Asian-cooking land, chocolate land, and snack land.

Our homes easily divide into zones, or lands. We have bedrooms (sleep land), kitchens (food land), utility rooms (laundry land), and so on. Principle #2 calls on us to clearly identify each zone by deciding which activity happens there, and then putting the tools we use therein, grouping them by common attributes. Let's look at some daily activities that call for zones, and what we would keep in those zones.

Sleep land: A bed's usually a good start here! Add whatever you need for sleeping—jammies, an eye pillow, an alarm clock, a bedside table and lamp. Our sleeping zone should be simple and restful. Anything that does not encourage a good night's sleep needs to live somewhere else. This includes large electronic equipment, such as televisions and computers, and stress-inducing reading materials—anything that feels like work instead of inspiration.

Some of you are going to argue that you like watching television in bed. Humor me. Remove the television and other large electronic devices from your bedroom for one week. If you truly notice no positive difference in how your room feels or how you sleep, then put the television back. But I think you'll like your room better without it!

Clothes land: Put everything you need to get dressed in one area—dresser, closet, jewelry display, mirror. Within these, organize your clothes, like with like. Usual categories include panties, bras, slips or undershirts, socks, stockings, casual short sleeve tops, casual long sleeve tops, casual pants, casual shorts, sweats, work/dress shirts—short and long sleeve—skirts, slacks, vests, sweaters, jackets, coats, shoes, scarves or ties, and hats. If you want to get really fancy, organize your clothes by color and patterns within these categories.

When hanging garments in the closet, put all the short clothes on one side and the long ones on the other side. This frees up space beneath the short items for shelving or shoe racks. Also, remember to use the walls. Shelving can be built into the sides of the closet; hats can be hung decoratively from hooks (or even nails). Jewelry or scarves can be hung along an inside closet wall, too.

Bath land: Usually called the bathroom, this is where we keep everything we need for bathroom activities. These can be segregated into mini-zones of bathing, grooming, brushing our teeth, storing our medicines, and using the toilet. Common item groupings include towels and wash cloths; body soaps; shampoo and conditioners; personal hygiene; tooth care; medicines and first aid; toilet paper; and supplies for cleaning the bathroom.

Food land: Also known as the kitchen. Here the zones break into the activities involved in keeping ourselves fed—food preparation, cooking, eating, clean-up, and storage. Ideally, our food is stored close to where it is prepared, as are our preparation tools—knives, cutting boards, mixing bowls, mixing spoons, and various appliances. Cooking tools such as pots, pans, hot pads, and spatulas should be close to the stove. Dishes can be stored either close to the sink or dishwasher for easy put-away, or close to the table for easy table setting. Table linens, candles and candle holders, and other items that increase our dining pleasure are best stored close to the table, perhaps in a nearby hutch or dresser.

Entertainment land: These days, most of our entertainment seems to be electronic. We therefore need zones for our televisions, VCRs, DVD players, CD players, tape decks, and turntables. Ideally, the equipment lives where we use it, which is usually a living room or family room. Close to these machines, we need homes for remote controls (labeled for easy identification), TV and radio program guides, videos, DVDs, CDs, tapes, and albums.

Not all entertainment is electronic, though. Some of us still play cards and board games. Games store nicely in closets or chests. If you use a card table, keep it folded and stored in the game closet. If it fits, you can even hang it from a couple of sturdy nails along the side or back of the closet to free up floor space.

Reading land: If you're like me, you have a hard time keeping your nose out of books. Furnish your reading zone with a good light, a comfortable chair (or chairs, if you read with others), a place to keep your beverage, and your reading materials. Magazine racks work well for containing magazines and newspapers that we are currently reading, but need to be weeded regularly (weekly?) so that only current reading lives there. Books traditionally live on bookshelves. Ideally, the reading zone is in the same room as the bookshelves, but this doesn't always work. If you are an avid reader, try to have at least a small bookshelf near your reading chair on which to store your current reading and to-be-read books.

A note on organizing books. My preference is to separate them into broad categories—e.g., fiction, poetry, children's, nonfiction, and reference (with subcategories for reference: health, gardening, writing, organizing)—and then to file them alphabetically by author within those categories. But this doesn't work for everybody. Some people prefer the visual aesthetics of organizing them by height, others by hardback vs. paperback, others by color, others by title. There is no right or wrong way to organize your books. What's important is that you are able to find a book when you want it. If you remember books by size and color (instead of by title or author), then that is how you should organize them.

Clearly, our homes contain a multitude of other zones: gifts and gift wrapping; laundry; computer; telephone; bill paying; travel;

camping; emergency supplies; pets; gardening.... For each of our activities, we want to create a zone in which everything associated with that activity is put together—like with like, based on function.

Little Bits of Paper

Our minds are held together by scraps of paper. Phone messages and important phone numbers, books we want to read and movies we want to see, tasks we want to accomplish, and everything else we don't want to forget—they all get scribbled down on the nearest empty envelope or yellow sticky. And then become promptly lost, or buried in a scattered pile on the kitchen counter, or tacked in a hodgepodge onto the bulletin board.

Maybe we should have a brain zone! I recommend two simple tools for gathering all these random must-not-forget thoughts into one place.

First, use a phone message pad. I like the flexibility of the two-part message pads because they let me tear off the top part and take it with me—a handy option when I want to bring along directions to a client's house, for example. But a simple notebook or pad of lined paper works well, too. Keep it by the phone (with a pen), and write down all phone messages on it. A check beside the message lets other household members know that you have seen it. A line through the message reminds you that it has been dealt with and can now be ignored.

The second tool is a notebook. Rather than jotting down notes on multiple pads or handy scraps, keep one—and only one—notebook for all your thoughts. You can divide it into sections to find your thoughts more readily if you choose, but it isn't necessary. Or you can use a computer, hand-held or otherwise. The point is to put all your information into one place. What matters is that the place you choose is easy for you to use.

Tasks

In the same way that we organize our things into like with like, we can organize our labor. Think of assembly lines for a moment. Obviously, we don't want to live our lives with the monotony of an assembly line, but we can use the concept of streamlining to make our lives easier. To this end, we want to group like tasks together. As an example, let's look at paying our bills (manually, not online). We can break the process into several steps. First we gather together the bills we plan to pay. Then we write the checks and enter them into our check register. Then we stuff the envelopes with the payment remittance and the check and seal the envelope. Then we address the envelopes (if not pre-addressed) and write our return address. Then we affix postage. Then we mail the payments. We also need to update the balance in our checkbook and file the paid bills.

Grouping tasks together makes sense. We don't wash each dish every time we dirty it; we wash the dishes. And we don't wash each individual garment every time we wear it; we wash the laundry. Other tasks can be batched together, too: paying our bills, filing, answering emails.

And running errands. Put errands together by location. I live in the countryside, and do my grocery shopping once a week in Arcata, which is about 25 minutes from my home. To minimize driving, I try to organize all my Arcata errands to correspond with my shopping day. Similarly, I try to coordinate all my Old Town (Eureka) errands into one trip. My ideal is to park my car in one central location, and then walk to all my errands from there.

Dear Claire:

My computer screen is covered with stickies — phone numbers, names, reminders. I can barely see the screen. Any suggestions? — Christine

Dear Christine:

I'd be willing to bet you can't see the stickies, either. Stickies (or Post-It® notes) work fine when there's one or two of them. When there are so many that your computer screen is covered, they stop being functional; they literally get lost in the crowd.

I suggest you keep a notebook handy and jot your notes into it instead of on stickies. Or use a two-part phone message pad. (This allows you to tear off the top sheet and place the information where you will actually use it.)

What kind of information is winding up on your computer screen? Phone numbers belong with the rest of your phone numbers. Rolodexes are a commonly used option. I use an index-card box because it lets me drop in phone numbers alphabetically even though they're on differently sized pieces of paper (business cards, phone messages, scrawlings on the back of grocery receipts, as well as those I've transferred neatly onto index cards). Or you may want to keep phone numbers in your computer (instead of on it).

Reminders are best transferred to a task-tracking system. The easiest is a "to-do" list. Other possibilities include writing reminders into your calendar, setting up and using a tickler system, or using a computerized scheduling program.

I'm not clear how you are using the names you jot onto stickies, so I'm not sure how you should handle them. Ask yourself why you are keeping them; the answer will direct you toward how to process them. It may be they can stay in the notebook where you originally wrote them down.

Having a book to note things into is great. But you also need to process the information, to put it away. Give yourself five or ten minutes every day to review your notes and handle them. Transfer phone numbers into your phone number system, add tasks to your to-do lists, review your notes to make sure you haven't forgotten something vitally important. Cross or check off items that have been processed. Circle a lone item that still needs to be handled so that it doesn't get overlooked.

By the way, bulletin boards often suffer from the same problem as your computer screen. Flyers, photos, business cards, scribbled notes—they all get tacked up in jumbled, overlapping chaos until there's so much paper on the board that nothing gets noticed, and the events you wanted to remember are forgotten for being buried. Bulletin boards are best used for current information, and are best accessed if kept neat. Give yourself a few minutes every now and then to maintain your board; take down out-of-date reminders, tidy what's there. And use the board; it does you no good if you don't refer to it.

I often suggest that clients examine their underlying beliefs and motives for their behaviors by asking, "what would happen if...? And then what? And then what?"

You might have fun exploring what you think would happen if you stopped covering your computer screen with stickies.

(I can hear it now: "If I no longer have stickies hiding my screen, I will be able to do my work. If I am able to do my work, then I'll have to do my work. If I have to do my work, then... ah, heck! I'll keep the stickies!")

Just don't cut out this letter and tape it to the monitor, okay?

A tickler system is where you put anything date related. It can be a 1-through-31 accordion file folder, 31 separate hanging file folders, or a desk-top box with 31 slots. (Some people also have a separate section for each month.) How to use a tickler? Put anything you want to remember for a specific date in that date's numbered section. For example, if you want to mail a birthday card on the 7th, put it in slot 7. Tickets to a show on the 22nd? Into slot 22. Dental appointment reminder card for the 15th? Into the spot labeled 15. Directions to a party on the 12th? Into number 12. The secret to a successful tickler is to check it *every* day.

3

K.I.S.S.

(Keep It Simple, Sweetie)

Out of clutter, find simplicity.

— *Albert Einstein*

Remember, being organized is about making our lives easier. The simpler we make our lives, the easier it is to stay organized.

Location, Location, Location

One trick to keeping our lives simple is to put things where we use them. Like water, we tend to take the path of least resistance. In other words, we're lazy. If we have to cross the room to put away a CD after playing it, chances are we won't make the effort. Instead, the CD will wind up in a pile—with other CDs we haven't put away—by the CD player. To avoid a jumbled pile of CDs, put the CD rack next to the player. This same concept applies to anything we can think of: reading glasses go by our reading chair; phone books by the telephone; cat litter by the cat box; fish food by the fish tank; spatulas by the stove.

If we have to work to reach an item or put it away, often we won't bother trying. Given our innate laziness, we need to assure that any tools or systems we implement are easy to access and use. This includes putting things we use most often in the easiest places to reach—what some organizers call "prime real estate." The far dark corner of the bottom kitchen cabinet where you've stacked your pots and pans is not a good home for your favorite pasta pot that you use every week. Instead, put it, along with other pots and pans that you cook with regularly, in front of the ones you use less often.

Prime use of "prime real estate" also entails putting those things we rarely need into the spaces that are harder to reach. Take, for example, those pesky cupboards above the refrigerator. While they are a good use of otherwise empty vertical space, they are not easy to reach. This makes them ideal storage for items that are used on rare occasions, perhaps the roasting pan for the once-a-year turkey, or large serving platters and bowls that are pulled out only for the occasional party.

Appropriately locating items is one aspect of K.I.S.S. Another aspect is ensuring that our tools are easy to use. In general, the more effort a tool requires, the less likely it will be used. Picture

a laundry hamper. If we have to lift the lid to put our dir
clothes inside, we're more likely to start a pile on top of t
hamper, not in it. An easier, and therefore more effecti
laundry hamper would be one that's open, so that we can to
our clothes in from across the room, if we so desire.

I've found the photo album to be another tool that just doesn't
work for me. While I like the idea of scrapbooking, the effort
required to pull out my supplies, lay out the page, trim the
decorations and photos, tape everything to the page, then wiggle
on the protective sleeve takes more energy and time than I'm
willing to expend on pictures. For me, a better tool is an acid-
free photo box with dividers. I can quickly pop a picture into its
section, and can just as quickly find any picture I want.

One, Two, Three...

The above example of storing photos illustrates another piece of
K.I.S.S.—minimize the number of steps that any process
requires. The more steps to a procedure, the more likely details
will fall through the cracks between the steps. Look at your
procedures and ask, "What is not essential to this process? What
can be eliminated?"

A psychotherapist I know had a complex system for processing
her bank deposits. For each check she received, the payment
needed to be recorded on the patient's ledger card; the copy of
the outstanding invoice was pulled from the accounts receivable
file, the check stub was stapled to it, and then both were two-
hole punched and placed in the patient's financial file; the
checks were stamp-endorsed; a bank deposit slip was prepared,
then photocopied along with each check; the name, amount
paid, and date of visit being paid for was recorded on the photocopy of the deposit; the photocopied checks and deposit were
three-hole punched and filed chronologically in the deposits
binder; the deposit amount was entered into the check register
and the bank balance was updated; and then, finally, the checks
were taken to the bank. (If you think that's exhausting to read,
imagine the tedium of preparing the deposit!)

...tually, the therapist switched over to an integrated accounting software program, saving numerous steps (and paper) as a result. Now, when she receives a check, she simply enters it into the computer, indicating it is payment for a specified invoice and, voilà! Her banking and receivables records are automatically updated. By saving to a disk, she eliminates the need for a paper trail. The only paper she uses, besides the checks, is the bank deposit slip. And the whole process takes one-quarter the time of her original procedure.

Little Bits of Time

My friend Robert tells a story about clearing the blackberries from his back yard. He would periodically muster his determination and tackle the prickly invaders, spending all day hacking away, ripping them out, until he was spent. He'd make significant progress, but would so wear himself out in the process that he was unable to re-muster his determination until much later, by which time the blackberries had returned. This futile battle continued, man against berry, until he remembered K.I.S.S. and changed tactics. He began to remove the berries one square yard at a time, slowly and methodically, until the entire patch had been eliminated.

Except for the lack of thorns, our cluttered homes resemble that yard of overgrown blackberry bushes. If I thought that I had to organize a client's entire house in one fell swoop, I'd probably crumple up and cry from anticipated exhaustion. Most organizing tasks are too big to tackle all at once; we shouldn't even try.

I limit my organizing sessions with clients to two-hour blocks because I've found anything more to be too tiring—for them as well as for me. If you are working on your own, or are just beginning, I recommend that you work in even smaller chunks—anywhere from 15 to 60 minutes. Decide in advance how long you will spend, then set a timer to let yourself know when to stop. By setting a limit, you are making a promise to yourself that you have to work for only so long; by setting the timer, you are helping yourself keep that promise. When you are first starting out, it is important that you learn to trust yourself, and that you build in experiences of success. You are learning a new set of skills, and need to extend the same compassion, patience, and encouragement to yourself that you extend to your children when they learn something new.

In order to facilitate a sense of accomplishment in a short amount of time, begin with a small area to organize, like a drawer. One drawer or cupboard at a time, eventually your entire home can become organized.

Take Breaks

Taking breaks functions on two fronts. When combined with working in small chunks, it prevents any job from becoming too big and too hard. Breaks help make a task more enjoyable and create feelings of success.

Taking a breather is especially important when we are working under tremendous pressure. It can feel counter-intuitive to pause. ("I can't stop now! I need to finish this report by 4:30!") And yet, this is exactly when a break is most helpful. When we step away from our work, we gain a fresh perspective on it, and return with renewed energy. The quality of our work actually improves when we take a break.

Give It a Name

While we're at it, let's give our memory a break, too. Instead of having to remember which shelf holds twin sheets and which holds queen, instead of having to

> "Every now and then go away, have a little relaxation. For when you come back to your work, your judgment will be surer, since to remain constantly at work, you lose power of judgment. Go some distance away, because then the work appears smaller and more of it can be taken in at a glance, and a lack of harmony or proportion is more readily seen."
> *Leonardo da Vinci*

remember which file drawer holds household finances and which has personal correspondence, we can use labels.

Many objects in our homes already have labels. Imagine the difficulty we'd have if there were no identifying labels—or titles—on books, records, tapes, CDs, videos, DVDs, or boxes of food. What a nuisance that would be, having to open every item to identify its contents!

Sometimes people object to the aesthetics of labels, thinking them unsightly. There are so many ways to create labels that this need not be a problem. Adhesive labels can be bought at any office supply store, including labels with decorative borders. Simple, attractive labels can be made with hand-held label-making machines. If you feel so inspired, you can embroider, appliqué, paint, draw, carve, or use calligraphy to make labels. You can even hide labels by putting them inside cupboards and drawers.

We can apply labels to many areas of our home. Some possible places for labels include:
- filing cabinet drawers
- file folders
- wall pockets for projects or household members
- closet shelves
- kitchen shelves
- bulk food containers (flour, spices, grains)
- homemade frozen and canned foods
- bookshelves
- dresser drawers
- art and crafts supplies
- storage items such as
    - holiday decorations
    - archived files
    - memorabilia being saved for children
- containers of camping equipment
- emergency supplies
- shelves and containers in children's rooms.

Labels are especially important for children who are learning to read. If you have children who are pre-literate, work with them to label the containers and shelves in their room. Make sure the categories make sense to your children (remember, children enjoy sorting and creating order), and come up with a simple name for each area. Then make a label that has both a picture of the category and the word, printed clearly. Do this together with your children. These labels will enable your young ones to put away their toys more easily, and will build literacy skills at the same time.

Of course, labels are good for children—and adults—who already know how to read, too. Whenever an area is clearly marked, it is easier for us to use. The less we have to remember, the more likely we are to successfully employ the systems we've put into place.

Clear Your Clutter

Clutter holds us back, depresses us, weighs us down, and blocks new experiences from flowing in. It also creates more work for us; the more stuff we have, the more we have to clean and take care of, and the more distracted we are by our environment. The less cluttered we make our surroundings, the simpler our lives become.

This doesn't mean we must get rid of everything and live a Spartan existence. We thrive with beauty and happy memories around us. It does mean we focus on finding balance by examining each item (and person, and commitment) and deciding whether or not it continues to be important to us.

Often, clearing space in our homes creates welcoming space in our lives. One story immediately comes to mind. Years ago, I knew a couple whom I'll call Keith and Carla. They had been dating for a while, were wonderfully compatible, and were in love. But Carla found herself unable to commit to the relationship so, to both their sorrow, she called for a trial separation. During this separation, Carla began to work on sorting and purging the contents of numerous boxes that had been cluttering her garage. As she let go of the accumulation of years of physical baggage, her psyche felt lighter, too. By the time she'd cleared out all those boxes, Carla was not only ready to start seeing Keith again, she was ready to marry him. (I had the honor of coordinating the food for their wedding.)

Clearing clutter is so important that the process deserves its own chapter. To learn the brass tacks of this process, see the chapter, "Clutter Clearing Made Easy."

Voluntary Simplicity

Simplicity has become the latest commercial fad. Even AOL-Time-Warner jumped on the bandwagon with its glossy publication, *Real Simple*, a magazine that exploits our longing for simplicity with advertising for a life that is anything but. In one issue, I counted 15 pages of ads before reaching the table of contents, 96 pages altogether in a 200-page magazine, including ads for diamonds, SUVs, and brand-name sunglasses. Real simple? Not in my book.

So what *does* it mean to live simply? According to Duane Elgin, a major figure in the Voluntary Simplicity movement, it means "choosing our path through life consciously, deliberately, and of our own accord. It's not so much about living with less as it is about living with purpose and balance.... The simple life is about freeing up time for what matters most to us."

A simple life is an examined life, where each aspect is a result of a concrete decision. When we choose a simple life, we choose to resist the pressures for materialistic consumerism. We choose to take back control of our lives, deciding how we live and what we buy. And our decisions are based in our values: simplicity, family, community, equality, beauty, honesty, justice, kindness, caring for the earth and all living creatures.

Small Is Beautiful

Choosing simplicity often results in scaling down our lives. We start to question each of our assumptions, examining whether they still apply to our lifestyle and values. We get to ask ourselves how many pairs of jeans and white blouses we really need, whether we use all those kitchen gadgets and power tools, whether we need the boat, RV, three cars, and two houses. We get to decide if our house fits us, if it is being used fully, or if we would be better off with a smaller, simpler home. We get to decide that keeping up with the Joneses is not what we want after all, and that a life lived true to our own values matters far more than what others may think of us.

Allow me to share my own life as an example of applied Voluntary Simplicity. My home is small, only 24 by 28 feet. While it lacks the impressive appearance of affluence that some of my clients' homes project, it is all I need. An unassuming clapboard cottage on the outside, inside my home is open and decorated with art and tchotchkes that I love. It is simple and welcoming, and fits me. Similarly, my car is not new or fancy, but it is

> "It shouldn't be surprising that in spending a lot of time [at malls], adolescents find little that challenges the assumption that the goal of life is to make money and buy products."
> from *The Malling of America*
>
> *Bill Kowinski*

comfortable, easy to drive, reliable, and gets respectable gas mileage. My wardrobe requires only three feet of closet space (compared to many women's wardrobes that fill multiple closets). I make frequent use of my public library, instead of owning every book I read. I attend plays on their opening discount night, movies during bargain matinées. My rider mower was originally on its way to the landfill because it had a broken steering pin and my neighbors had bought a new mower rather than fix this one. They offered it to me, my sweetie fixed it for $17.00, and it's been running since. Cable does not run out to my home, but I prefer not to watch television rather than spend money on a satellite service. Similarly, I do not purchase most of the extra services offered by my phone company. I eat very little prepared food, opting to buy organic products in bulk and do my own cooking. My cleaning supplies are simple—Bon Ami cleanser, baking soda, vinegar—and I don't bother buying plastic garbage bags; plastic and paper grocery bags work fine for garbage. When I travel, I camp, stay in hostels, or with friends.

In other words, I'm a lousy consumer. But I do not feel deprived. Rather, I find pleasure in living simply. Because I live small, I have more time, more energy, and need less money to live a life personalized to me. It is easier to keep my life organized, because I keep it simple. In fact, I'd argue that Voluntary Simplicity is the ultimate manifestation of "Keep It Simple, Sweetie."

> "Garbage production is crucial to a market economy. American capitalism hinges on our willingness to keep producing trash. ... As the 1950s wore on, most people already owned what they needed. The producers responded with "built-in obsolescence." Companies like General Electric began making products such as toasters and light bulbs that were designed to wear out, styles began to change more rapidly, and totally new "needs"—electric can openers, fabric softener—were invented. As Vance Packard pointed out in his 1960 bestseller, *The Waste Makers*, innovation in products was replaced with a parade of different and not necessarily improved styles. ...
>
> Capitalist growth and profitability depend as much on the destruction of wealth as on the production of it. While salvaging the value contained in a discarded but perfectly usable desk is rational from an environmental and social point of view, it is irrational and not useful for the furniture industry, which must produce and sell more and more desks in order to thrive. Ultimately, the environmental crisis, of which garbage is just a subset, is inseparable from the logic of our whole economic system." *Heather Rogers and Christian Parenti*

Dear Claire:

I collect recipes. Cooking magazines, recipes torn out of the newspaper, recipes on scraps of paper, cookbooks... How do I organize this mess? — K.

Dear K:

Sigh. Aren't recipes fun? All those nummy-looking dishes shown in the magazines. Someday we'll make them, right? So we hold on to magazine after magazine, clipping upon clipping, one cookbook after another.

Most of us rarely try even half of the recipes we've collected. We need to be realistic, to sort and purge. Our cooking styles and needs change. Do we have the time, energy, or inclination to cook elaborate meals? No? Then out go those recipes. Can we still eat those high-fat, high-cholesterol desserts? Dang! No... out they go. On the other hand, that recipe for a quick, low-fat, one-dish meal is worth trying.

Sort according to your cooking style and dietary needs. Also sort by success. Some recipes are tried and true, and are worth keeping. Others are recipes you honestly will try sometime soon. And then there's that recipe for "Homard à la Vierge à la Mémoire de Dom Perignon" that you clipped in 1990 and still haven't tried, because you never, ever, bought French champagne and lobsters and you probably never will.

Sorting is one thing, storage and retrieval another. "How do I organize this mess?" you asked. Well, the classic method is with an index box. Dot Hobson, my beloved neighbor when I was growing up, typed all her recipes onto 3 x 5 cards and filed them in an index box, kept handily on her kitchen counter. This works well if you have the time and focus to transfer all your recipes to index cards. Frankly, I don't.

Organizing is about making life as easy as possible. I want a system where I can toss things and be able to find them when I need them. So I devised a simple system for all my loose recipes. I bought a loose-leaf binder and a packet of pocketed manila dividers. On each pocket I wrote a category based on how I think of my recipes (in alphabetical order): beans; bread, savory; bread, sweet; cakes; cookies; fish; fruit desserts; meat; muffins; pies; poultry; sauces; soups; vegetable main dishes; and vegetable side dishes. I also have a pocket for miscellaneous health information, and one for recipes for Passover (because these have specific dietary requirements). You might want one for Thanksgiving, or hors d'oeuvres.

Another possible category is To Be Tried. That way, only the tested recipes are filed into their appropriate pockets, and the recipes you want to try are waiting patiently at the front of your binder. If this pocket starts bulging, you know something has to shift. Either you need a reality check (am I really going to try all of these recipes?) or you need to create time to cook. Once a week (or once a month), flip through the To Be Tried recipes, choose one, buy the ingredients, and make it.

Some people use their computers to organize their recipes. If your computer is easily accessible from the kitchen, and if entering recipes into your computer is something you enjoy and will actually do, then by all means, knock yourself out. Software that works with scanners is available to organize your recipes. And saving to disk certainly reduces the paper mess. There are also myriad Web sites available for finding recipes.

Between index cards, computers, and binders, you should have a working option for your loose recipes. Now, on to those magazines and cookbooks. First, remember to think vertical: store them upright, like books on a library shelf. You can buy holders to contain your magazines. Next, purge. Reduce your magazine subscriptions to one or two that you truly love and use, and keep only the current year. If there are recipes in back issues that you have tried and will use again, tear them out, file them with your other loose recipes, then recycle the rest of the magazine. Go through your cookbooks. If there are only one or two recipes in the whole book that you use, copy them down, then get rid of the book. If you don't use it and love it, pass it on to someone who will.

Can't remember which cookbook that recipe is in? Write down the name of the recipe, the cookbook, and the page number it's on, then file this with your loose recipes under the appropriate category. Or have a page in the beginning of your binder where you write down this information.

As always when organizing, start with your current stack, then make your way through your backlog. And ask for help. Having someone with you can help you stay focused and make clear decisions, avoiding the black holes of nostalgia ("Oh, I remember this recipe!") and daydreaming (where you intend to glance at a cookbook and find yourself still reading it 20 minutes later). The All-American Cowboy Cookbook is a lot of fun, but will you really make anything from it?

4

Create,

and Use,

Habits and Schedules

Always leave enough time in your life to do something that makes you happy, satisfied, even joyous. That has more of an effect on economic well-being than any other single factor.

— Paul Hawken

Habits and schedules provide routine to our lives, and routine provides structure. Without structure, we are left free-floating in a vast ocean, exposed to the elements and the whims of the currents. With structure, we have a boat that contains us, protecting us to some degree from the capriciousness of our surroundings.

Or, to switch metaphors, routine saves us from having to repeatedly recreate the wheel. Once we figure out what works for us, we can reuse it, rather than inventing it fresh each time.

Daily Routines

Mornings are a prime example of the need for routines. Even though I am a "morning person," I find it difficult to get out of bed without a game plan, an idea of what to do once I arise. Without a routine, I am likely to putter away for hours, hanging out with the cats, poking around the Internet, reading a book, forgetting to eat breakfast or get dressed until after noon. Of course, sometimes this is okay. We all need downtime, unstructured opportunities to putter and relax.

But I prefer not to spend every morning in unstructured lounging; I feel like I'm wasting my life if I putter very often. So I have created a morning routine for myself. I get up (usually upon the insistent demands of five hungry cats) and immediately make my bed. I then tend to pet and house chores: I open the curtains, tidy the couch cushions, feed the fish and cats, clean the cat box, sweep the floors, shower, dress, fix and eat breakfast, clear the dishes, and wipe off the counters and stove. On garbage day, I take out the garbage. If I need to bring in firewood, I do so before sweeping the floors.

This is the skeletal structure, a flexible framework for my mornings. The rest of my morning depends upon what I have planned for the day. If I have a morning client, I pack a lunch and skedaddle out the door. If my morning is open, I turn on the computer to check email and read my all-time favorite columnist, Jon Carroll. Depending upon mood and need, I also use my mornings to write, pay bills, or handle business matters through the mail or by telephone.

Many other areas of our lives can also benefit from implementing routines. For example, I go grocery shopping once a week, typically on Saturdays because that is when my favorite farmers' market is held throughout half the year, and the market is one block away from my favorite grocery store. (Because of delivery schedules, it is also when the produce is freshest at the store.) Before leaving for market—water bottles, washed plastic bags, and canvas shopping bags in tow—I take a quick inventory of my food supplies (an easy task because they are all organized according to Principle #2: like with like). I also thumb through my cookbooks for ideas on what to cook that week. Using these ideas and my inventory, I jot down a shopping list on a piece of scratch paper, noting which dishes I intend to make and roughly grouping items together by where they are located in the store.

> Grant me the ability to be alone.
>
> May it be my custom to go
>
> outdoors each day
>
> among the trees and grasses,
>
> among all growing things
>
> and there may I be alone,
>
> and enter into prayer
>
> to talk with the one
>
> that I belong to.
>
> *Rabbi Nachman of Bratzlav*

I also have a routine for my housework, although it is very flexible. Such chores as laundry, vacuuming, dusting, and cleaning the bathroom wind up being done weekly, although I have not been consistent about which day of the week they get done. Rather, I do them on an as-needed basis. Some people prefer to set aside one day each week for housework, but I get tired if I clean the whole house in one session, so I do a different chore each day. (This is K.I.S.S. applied to housework!)

Tidy Up

One chore, however, should be done daily: we need to pick up and put things away every day. Luckily, Principles #1 through #3 teach us how to determine the right place for every object. Now all we have to do is create the time and habit of putting away our tools and toys. Doing so is essential if we are to maintain the organizational systems we've implemented.

At work, we need to stop 10 to 20 minutes before quitting time so that we can reorganize our work area. If we can't stop early, then we should invest in ourselves by staying a few minutes late. Being greeted by the serenity and sanity of an organized work area is worth the extra few minutes spent putting our space in order.

At home, we can clean up after each activity (such as clearing the dishes after a meal), or we can allot 10 to 30 minutes each evening to picking up and putting away our mess from the day.

One client tells a funny story. She had been bemoaning her chronic disorganization at a support group when someone suggested she hire a professional organizer, giving her my name and number. Sometime later, she was again complaining to a friend. Pulling out a piece of paper from her coat pocket, she lamented, "Look how disorganized I am! Here's a phone number, and I have no idea who this person is!" Her friend laughed. "That's the professional organizer." Indeed, it was my name and number in her coat pocket.

Moral of the story? When you write down a phone number, make sure you put down the person's name and why you want to call them.

Some daily put-away tasks include:

♦ purchases, such as books, music, and office supplies
♦ groceries
♦ items in our car, such as water bottles, lunch boxes, and
  papers
♦ mail and other paperwork
♦ reading materials
♦ clothing, clean laundry
♦ toys.

If we have children, we should involve them in this daily pickup time. Make sure you have demonstrated how to pick things up and where to put them away, though. Children need to be shown specifically what you expect of them; "Clean up your room!" is as vague—and unsuccessful—a command as "Be good."

A Place for Everything, and Everything in Its Place

Once an appropriate home has been designated for an item, it is easy to put that item back. Designated homes also help us to find items. How much time have we lost looking for our keys, our glasses, our purse? How often have we paid late fees because we couldn't find our bills to pay them on time? How often have we lost respect because we were disorganized? Searching for misplaced items costs us. On the other hand, consistently putting our important objects in the same places each time saves us time, money, stress, and embarrassment. Consistency is key.

But where should we put our keys? Where they make sense. Some people have key hooks on the wall by the door. Others have a bowl or basket by the door, on the kitchen counter, or on their dresser. I keep mine in a specific section of my purse. There is no right place to keep your keys; what matters is only that they are always in the same place, and that that place makes sense to you.

Time Is on My Side

We develop habits to make it through our day, to tidy up at the end, and to keep ourselves from losing important objects (and our minds). We can also habitualize our time by creating schedules. Now, before you react with panic at the thought of a minute-by-minute schedule that feels like a yellow-and-blue power tie constricting your neck, remember: organization is a tool that supports us in our life journey. We can "tie up" our time as loosely as we want. Our goal is to provide ourselves with enough structure to make life easy, not to squeeze the joy out of it.

Plenty of books have been written about time management. My intent here is to give you a simple guideline for creating a schedule for yourself, not to replicate the detailed (and often complex) systems found in other books.

The Right Tool for the Job

First, most people benefit from keeping a calendar. If your life is very routine, with only the occasional dental appointment or theater engagement to remember, then an attractive wall or desk calendar is usually sufficient. If you need to keep track of multiple appointments or activities—lunch dates, business meetings, client sessions, soccer practice, yoga classes—a calendar with preprinted time slots is more helpful.

I suggest writing your engagements in pencil. Guaranteed, plans change, and pencil is much easier to erase than pen. If you are keeping a family calendar, use a different color of pencil for each family member, and keep the colored pencils (and an eraser) by the communal calendar.

Of course, you can eliminate pencils and erasers by choosing a PDA (Personal Digital Assistant). In the debate between Palm vs. Paper, neither side wins hands down. There are advantages and disadvantages to both systems, including their costs, complexity, and learning curves. If you think you might be interested in a PDA, I recommend that you research them, including speaking to people who use them, before making a purchase. PDAs are wonderful tools for many people, and a complete waste of money for others.

No matter whether we use a calendar, date book, PDA, or some other tool for recording our appointments, the tool is useless if we forget to consult it. Memory is fallible, as the following example shows.

I usually schedule clients from 10:00 to noon, and from 2:00 to 4:00. I keep a fairly regular schedule, but I'm not rigid; I try to work around my clients' needs. One day, I worked with my morning client from 10:00 to noon, then drove to the water-front for my lunch break. I ate my PB&J sandwich, finished reading a short story by Ursula LeGuin, drank a decaf mocha at a coffee shop, and waited until it was time for my 2:00 p.m. client. Finally, I drove up to her house, glanced at my calendar... and crumbled. We had scheduled to meet from 1:00 to 3:00. Oh, no! Naturally, I apologized profusely, offered to work the last hour for free, took responsibility for my error. Luckily, my mistake worked well for her; she had used the time to work on a pressing project, and was grateful for it.

Memory is unreliable. That's why we have systems. But we have to use them. When we rely on habits and memory alone, we blow it. So learn with me from my mistake—check your calendar daily.

Plugging in the Pieces

A while back there was an inspirational piece circulating on the Internet called "Big Rocks." Its message was that we need to schedule in the "big rocks" of our life—important factors like love, family, and spirituality—before trying to squeeze in all the piddly little details that usually fill our time. Just about every time-management expert tells us the same thing: we must take care of ourselves, make time for our highest values.

But first we need to identify our values. So, what's important to you? Fantasize for a moment. Grab pen and paper, and jot down all the things you like to do. (Yes, right now.) Next, write down what an ideal day would look like. If you're feeling overwhelmed with your life, you might be tempted to describe a perfect vacation day. This is good information, but you also want to be realistic by writing down an ideal normal day, something you can sustain on a regular basis.

Now look at what you've written. What stands out as important? Walking in the woods? Cooking tasty meals for friends? Curling up with a whodunit? Roller-skating? Writing the great American novel? Grown-up time with your partner? Attending religious services? Meditating? Exercising at the gym? Going to the kids' games? Helping the kids with their homework? Reading them a bedtime story? Working on your doctoral thesis? Taking naps with the cats?

The answers will be different for each of us. Whatever they are, though, we need to honor them. We need to schedule them into our life. No "yes, buts" allowed. As George Bernard Shaw pointed out, "People are always blaming their circumstances for what they are. I don't believe in circumstances. The people who get on in this world are the people who get up and look for the circumstances they want and, if they can't find them, make them."

So let's get to work, plugging in the pieces. Draw a simple table, Monday through Sunday across the page, and your waking hours down the page. Now look at your list of what's important to you. Let's pretend the list includes going to the gym, helping the kids with their schoolwork, spending quality time with your partner, meditating, walking outdoors, attending religious services, learning a foreign language, reading recreationally, and working 9 to 5 at a job that has a half-hour commute in each direction. Quite a lot of activities to schedule in!

The first step is to look at the biggest time commitment and explore if there is a way to lessen it. This would be your 9 to 5 job and its attendant commute. Can you change your hours to a four-day week, or work part-time, perhaps by job-sharing? Can you telecommute? Can you take public transportation instead of driving? Can you change jobs to something that requires fewer hours or is closer to home?

Next, fill in the table, starting with activities whose times are predetermined. Let's assume you've explored your options and, for now, your job is not flexible. Go ahead and block off on the table the time you are at work (but leave your lunch hour open). Next, fill in the time for church services. Now, decide with your partner when you would like to be together, *sans* offspring. One popular solution is to hire a babysitter one night a week, say Wednesday. So fill in Wednesday evenings after work for a date with your sweetie. Monday, Tuesday, and Thursday evenings can be marked as time with the kids, from after dinner until their bedtime.

This leaves mornings before work, your commute time, your lunch break, Friday evenings, Saturdays, and Sundays free (excepting time at church). Granted, you may have to go to bed earlier so that you can get up earlier. But if meditating and going to the gym are important to you, then it is worth shifting your sleep patterns slightly. So, write in going to the gym before work on Monday, Wednesday, and Friday mornings. As long as you're getting up early, you can block off Tuesday and Thursday mornings for meditating or taking a walk. Your lunch breaks should be true breaks from work; you can use the time to meditate, read, walk, have lunch with a friend (or your sweetie), or study your foreign language lessons. If you find that you are using your lunch breaks to run errands, you can schedule in your more important activities (meditating, reading) to prevent errands from usurping every lunch break. You can also use your commute time to practice mindfulness (let every red light be a reminder to breathe!), or listen to books on tape, language tapes, inspirational tapes, or educational tapes. Or, if you take public transportation (and can read in a moving vehicle without becoming sick), you can also use your commute for recreational reading.

As you plug in various activities, include two oft-overlooked pieces: time for transition and maintenance. Time at the gym means more than your workout; it includes travel to and from the gym, getting into your workout clothes, stretching, showering, and getting dressed. Morning prep includes clearing up after breakfast and hanging up the clothes you tried on, then tore off, in your quandary over what to wear today. (Laying out your clothes the night before only works if you live somewhere with consistently predictable weather.) Dinnertime includes dishwashing; evening kid time includes evening pickup. Your driving commute should allow time for unexpected traffic, hitting every red light between here and there, searching for a parking place, and then walking from your car to your destination. Meetings need to be scheduled with time in between so you can put away your notes from one meeting, prepare your thoughts for the next one, have a comfortable amount of time to travel from one to the next, and a few moments (at least) in which to re-center yourself.

And so, activities, transition, and maintenance time in place, your schedule would look something like the table on the next page.

Wow! You have time to do everything you said you wanted, with open time left over. Now, resist the temptation to fill in the open time with additional commitments. You need leisure (or "open") time to nurture yourself: to go to a movie or a party, on a picnic or a hike; to get a massage; soak in a hot tub; attend a meditation retreat or writing workshop; hang out at the river all day; or putter in your garden.

Remember, this schedule is yours, created to provide structure for your life. As such, it is changeable. This schedule gives you a guideline, helps you make decisions about when you will do what. And you can choose to change it anytime you want. Nothing is carved in stone.

	Monday	Tuesday	Wednesday	Thursday	Friday	Saturday	Sunday
6 a.m.	gym	meditate/walk	gym	meditate/walk	gym	OPEN	▶
7 a.m.	prep	prep	prep	prep	prep	▶	▶
8:30 a.m.	commute	commute	commute	commute	commute	▶	▶
9 a.m.	work	work	work	work	work	▶	▶
10 a.m.	▶	▶	▶	▶	▶	▶	church
11 a.m.	▶	▶	▶	▶	▶	▶	▶
12 p.m.	errands	study	walk	study	friends	▶	family
1 p.m.	work	work	work	work	work	▶	projects/
2 p.m.	▶	▶	▶	▶	▶	▶	fun
3 p.m.	▶	▶	▶	▶	▶	▶	▶
4 p.m.	▶	▶	▶	▶	▶	▶	▶
5 p.m.	commute	commute	commute	commute	commute	▶	▶
6 p.m.	dinner	dinner	date	dinner	dinner	▶	dinner
7 p.m.	kids	kids	with	kids	open	▶	open
8 p.m.	▶	▶	sweetie	▶	▶	▶	▶
9 p.m.	read to kids	read to kids	▶	read to kids	▶	▶	▶
10 p.m.	bedtime	bedtime	bedtime	bedtime	bedtime	▶	bedtime

Dear Claire:

I noticed you are doing some workshops on the paper storm. I am especially interested in learning what to save, for how long, and what to toss. Phone bills? Save or toss? — Tracy

Dear Tracy:

What you keep requires knowing why you are keeping it. Start by asking, "Why am I keeping this? How do I plan to use it?"

"I might need it for my taxes, but I'm not sure," is a common response. To be sure, I spoke with Robert Sutter, CPA with Jackson & Eklund in Arcata, California. His criterion is, "How long can the government go back and look at records?" The federal limit for conducting an audit (unless they suspect fraud, which has no limits) is three years; for California, it's five years. He advises clients to keep supporting tax documents for five years. (Keep actual tax returns, without receipts and other supporting information, indefinitely, in case the IRS says you didn't file in a given year.) Supporting records include receipts for business expenses and itemized deductions, and proof of all income (including bank statements). If you have a business calendar, keep this with your tax records, too.

Everyone has his or her own tax-preparation style. Some people update their financial records monthly. Others throw everything into a shoebox and deal with it on April 14. If you have a business, I strongly recommend monthly—or at least quarterly—profit and loss statements. If you have a lot of financial activity, I again suggest regular record keeping. But if your tax records are fairly simple, toss the information into a "Current Year Taxes" folder or envelope. Organize the information in January. (Schedule a date with yourself.) When your W-2s and other statements come, plug in the figures and file your taxes. Or be organized early for your accountant, saving everyone time and you money.

Where to store past tax records? Set six hanging files in a file box or drawer. In the front hanging file, place all your tax returns chronologically, most recent in front. In the remaining five files, store all the supporting documents for your returns, one year in each file (again, most recent in front). When you file taxes next year, empty the oldest (rear) file, shredding the supporting documents. Put the supporting documents for the new year's taxes into the file you just emptied and move that file to the front. Voilà, you again have information for your five most recent returns in chronological order. Repeat this process every year.

Let me give you an example. If you were to set up this system in 2005, your files would look like this: Tax Returns, Supporting Documents for 2005, 2004, 2003, 2002, and 2001. The following year you would empty the 2001 file, move it up front, and put supporting documents for 2006 in it, so that the files would now be ordered as Tax Returns, Supporting Documents for 2006, 2005, 2004, 2003, and 2002. (The actual return for 2006 would be filed in the front of the Tax Returns file.)

In addition to keeping tax returns, keep records that relate to investments—stocks, property, houses—for as long as you own the investment, plus five years after liquidating the investment. The same advice holds for mortgage and loan documents.

Other keepers include: automobile records (title, registration, repairs); household inventory, appraisal, and repair records; current insurance policies; current passport; receipts for appliances, art, antiques, or other major purchases; warranties and instruction manuals. Save all of these for as long as they are current. Vital records—adoption, birth, marriage, divorce, death, wills, documentation of copyrights and patents—should be kept permanently.

Keep ATM and credit card slips in envelopes (labeled by bank or credit card account) with your "to be paid" items. When the statement arrives, match them up to make sure you were charged or credited correctly. If you made a tax-deductible purchase with your credit card, file the slip with your tax records. Otherwise, file the slips with the paid statements. ATM slips, once reconciled, can be shredded.

As for phone and utility bills, my preference, probably because I was a bookkeeper for many years, is to keep my bills, filed by vendor, for the current year. But this isn't necessary. Many folks keep them for just one month, until the next bill arrives. Ask yourself, "Do I need to own this personally, or can I access it elsewhere?" Often, if we need a copy of a bill, we can get it from the company. I keep my phone bills because they are a partial tax deduction. Otherwise, I don't need to keep my paid bills; I just like to. Your choice will depend upon your needs.

If an item has expired, is not needed for taxes or to document child support expenses, and doesn't serve some other redeeming or legal purpose, toss it. Expired coupons, announcements to past events (oops, missed that one!), grocery receipts, junk mail, duplicates, instructions for the toaster that died last year... out they go. Remember to ask, "Why am I keeping this? How do I plan to use it?" "I don't know" is not an acceptable answer. Nor is, "I might need it someday." If, after reading this answer, you still aren't sure, take Robert Sutter's final piece of advice, "When in doubt, call your friendly accountant."

5

Be Realistic

It is my observation that too many of us are spending money we haven't earned to buy things we don't need to impress people we don't like.

— Ken Blanchard

Years ago, I lived with a man who could fix or build anything. This skill served him in good stead; for example, just as he was becoming serious about his ceramics work, he found a discarded kiln that he was able to repair and use for his artwork. However, being able to fix anything had its drawbacks, too. Every repairable object became a potential treasure, another project. Eventually I put my foot down, insisting that he not bring home any more projects until he'd completed some of the ones already waiting for his attention. Yes, I agreed, that rocking chair would be wonderful if it were re-caned, but when are you going to re-cane it, and where will you put it until then?

Many of my clients—particularly the artists—exhibit a similar enthusiasm for the world around them. Everything becomes a potential art project; the world is one large creative masterpiece waiting to be manifested. Corks, pull tabs, shells, rocks, pieces of yarn, pictures in magazines... all are potential art. I think it's great that people can see the world with such wonder and creativity. The trick is to organize the materials so that they are accessible, and to be honest with oneself about the ramifications of owning the materials.

Being realistic means asking and honestly answering a few reality-check questions. These questions can be applied to things, people, and time commitments with equal efficacy. If you need to, copy them down and keep them in your wallet, or post them where you'll see them every day—on your mirror or refrigerator, for instance. Keep them in front of you until you have memorized them and trained yourself to apply them before making any decision.

Reality Check

◆ Can I afford it? (Remember to include maintenance costs.)
◆ Where will I put it?
◆ How long will this take, including preparation, clean up, and travel time?
◆ Is it in keeping with my goals and values?
◆ Do I even like it?

Clearly, being realistic is most challenging when we must decide about matters that matter to us. It's easy enough to know that you don't want to buy season tickets to the opera when you don't even like opera. But what happens when you're faced with making decisions about things you cherish?

Let's look at three possible scenarios.

1. You are asked to serve on the board of directors of your favorite nonprofit organization.

2. The *cutest* puppy is being given away in front of the supermarket. The kids giving away the puppy say that, if they can't find a home for it by this evening, their parents will take it to the pound.

3. Mom and Dad are scaling down, getting rid of half their belongings so that they can move into smaller quarters now that the kids are grown. They do not want to move Grandma's furniture, and they offer it to you.

Time to pull out the reality-check questions.

Can I afford it? What costs are involved in volunteering? Probably not much more than transportation and an occasional meal. Puppies, however, do entail a pretty outlay of pennies. This little darling is going to require a checkup, vaccinations, and being neutered, as well as food, a collar and leash, maybe a doghouse, and who knows how much to replace shoes and other unfortunate teething toys. As for Grandma's furniture, the biggest cost will be moving it, with maybe a bit to maintain it. (This assumes that no repairs are needed.) Depending upon its value, you may also choose to insure it.

Where will I put it? In the case of a volunteer commitment, this question refers to your schedule. How are you going to fit this activity into your week? The puppy's space needs apply to its food and water dishes, its bedding, and room to exercise. This question particularly applies to Grandma's furniture, though.

Where *are* you going to put the armoire? The couch? The dressers and lamps and dining room table with matching chairs? Are you going to get rid of your current furniture to make room for hers? Do you have room to mix it in with your existing furnishings? Or will you need to rent a storage unit and, if so, for how long and at what cost?

How long will this take, including preparation, clean up, and travel time? You're told that the board of directors meets for two hours, twice a month. You could handle four hours a month. But is this all you are committing to? What about commuting to and from the meetings? What about the fact that the board president never keeps to the schedule, so that meetings routinely run late? What about the additional duties expected of you as a board member? How long is this really going to take? Similarly, that puppy has hidden time costs. She'll need time to walk and play, time to be loved, fed, bathed, picked up after. Grandma's furniture will need to be dusted and polished.

Is it in keeping with my goals and values? If your goal is to have more time for family and fun, then volunteering as a board member is not a good idea. If, however, your goal is to become more active in your community, to be of service to others, or to add experience that may benefit your career, then volunteering could be just the thing. If you've been longing for a canine companion, then that puppy may be a godsend. But if you have four dog-hating cats at home and value your serenity, or if you are planning a six-month trip around the world, then you may be better off without a puppy. If you prefer to live with minimal possessions, you might opt to say "no thanks" to Mom and Dad's offer. However, if you yearn to decorate your home with antiques, Grandma's furniture might be what you've been looking for.

Do I even like it? Yes, you like the nonprofit, and you'd like to be of service, but the thought of serving on a board of directors sends uncomfortable shivers down your spine. You'd much rather volunteer as a literacy tutor. And yes, it is the cutest puppy, which might go to the pound if you don't take it, but you really don't want the responsibility of caring for and training a dog. As for Grandma's furniture, well, you loved Grandma but, man, did she have lousy taste.

One other question comes to mind, one I find myself asking of others on a regular basis. That is, "*When* will we do it?" When will we take the defunct computer equipment that's been sitting behind our couch for a year to the computer recycling company? When will we transplant the catnip into a hanging pot so that the cats don't mangle it? When will we call the doctor to make an appointment for our annual exam? It's fine to have good intentions, but they need to be grounded in reality. They need to be given a time and date to be made real.

To Thine Own Self Be True

Being realistic also means knowing oneself. What's that saying, "The road to hell is paved with good intentions"? It's good to place a time and date on our intentions, but the appointments need to be ones that we can honestly keep.

I'm going to pick on a very dear friend of mine for a moment, because he is such a good example of being unrealistic. Let's call him George.

George lives alone with four cats and a 50-gallon aquarium of freshwater fish, attends the community college full-time where he studies landscaping, and supports himself as a part-time gardener.

George is not a morning person. He tends to be easily distracted, has difficulty accurately estimating how long a project takes (partially because he thinks only of the activity, forgetting about preparation and cleanup), and has to work extra hard and long to succeed at school. (He is also bright, creative, funny, and caring, and makes a wonderful friend.)

So what does George do? He signs up for an 8:00 a.m. Plant Biology class, insisting he'll make himself go. Or he decides that he can get up early one morning to clean the aquarium, which takes him a minimum of two hours. Or he postpones writing his term paper until the night before it is due. Oy!

What George does is deny his natural tendencies and, in the process, sets himself up for repeated failure. Because you know that he didn't make it to that 8:00 a.m. class and wound up dropping it, and that the aquarium didn't get cleaned that week, and that he stayed up until all hours and still didn't finish the paper on time, losing points on an "A" paper because it was turned in late.

George is by no means unique in his denial and subsequent self-sabotage. I'm guessing we all have some area in our life where we are less than totally honest with ourselves, where we could use practice being realistic. It seems that one last question should be added to our reality check: "Am I really going to do it?"

Dear Claire:

I want to move. The kids are gone; the town has become too crowded. But I have 30 years of accumulated stuff in this house. I need to get rid of a lot of it before I can move, but just thinking about it exhausts me. I guess I should be ruthless and throw things away, but... Where do I begin? — Fanny

Dear Fanny:

Welcome to the empty nest. Several of my clients are in a similar situation. Their needs have changed and they want to scale down, but they feel overwhelmed and unsure where to start.

You are at a time of transition. So take stock. What is important to you now? What do you want and need in your life? Make a list. Maybe you used to entertain and no longer wish to. Or maybe you want to finally entertain now that the kids are gone. Do you want to have a guest room? A home office? What do you need for your hobbies and interests? How big a home do you want to take care of?

One of my clients asked herself, "If I had to move tomorrow, what would I take with me?" She then went through her belongings, keeping only the most meaningful: a pair of earrings her son gave her, a favorite chair and lamp, the portrait of her grandmother.

As you answer these questions, create a list of what you need and want in your life, then eliminate the excess. How many dishes do you really need? How many chairs and beds and sets of bedding? (The rule of thumb on bedding, by the way, is two complete sets for each regularly used bed, and one set for each guest bed.) How many tables and desks and sweaters and shoes and...? You get the idea.

As for the issue of exhaustion, I recommend taking it slowly and in small chunks.

Once you have your list, begin sorting and discarding the extras in your life. Take it a half-hour, maybe an hour, at a time. Focus on only one room or category. Structure your tasks so that, at the end of each period, you feel as though you've accomplished something. For example, one night you might sort the linen closet, choosing the sheets and towels you want to keep, and emptying the closet of the rest. It's a good idea to have some place (other than the floor or bed) to put things as you sort. The keepers probably already have homes—linens in the linen closet, dishes in the cupboards, clothes in the dresser and closet, etc. But what about the rest? Set up three boxes or paper bags each time you sort: garbage, give-away, and I-don't-know. Store these in an out-of-the-way staging area, perhaps in a guest room or the garage. Make the sorting process as non-intrusive as you can. Keep the clutter and chaos to a minimum.

I encourage you to recycle what you don't keep. Recycling includes giving items to your kids, charitable causes, and friends; having a yard sale; and taking items to the recycling center nearest you. Recycling is a great way to "share the wealth;" as they say, "one person's trash is another person's treasure."

A client once joked that I should advertise as follows: "Want to lose weight? Hire an organizer!" Culling through your belongings is like losing weight. It works best when done slowly and consciously, with the support of others. When you see only the sum total of 30 years in one house, the process naturally feels daunting! But if you take this weight loss in small tasks, one project and one day at a time, you can do it. With patience, compassion for yourself, conscious choices, and support from a professional organizer, you can whittle that 30 years of stuff down to a manageable—and movable—life.

6

Set Boundaries

Growth for the sake of growth is the ideology

of a cancer cell.

— *Edward Abbey*

Despite the popularity of the "Just say no" slogan, many people still find it difficult to do so. Therefore, when I teach about setting boundaries at my workshops, I have my students practice saying "No, thank you!" in unison. Even I have my weaknesses when it comes to setting boundaries; as I type these words, a 12-week-old kitten is curled, purring, upon my shoulder, because I haven't the heart to keep removing him. Even the fact that he lives with me demonstrates my unwillingness to say *no* to a kitten who comes mewing to my home, lost and hungry.

Of course, we don't need to say *no* every time, but we do need to say *no* when appropriate. Without boundaries, our lives become formless, unsupported—water without a bowl to contain it.

Boundaries take many shapes and sizes. They can be placed around time, people, and things. Saying *no* is one way to set boundaries. Erecting barriers, be they a closed door or a safety margin of time, is another. Containers are a third.

Say No with a Smile

More than just about anything else, people complain to me about unwanted solicitations—junk mail, junk phone calls, junk email. While it may be impossible to stop all unwelcome sales pitches, you can certainly slow down the onslaught. Here are some things you can do for free.

♦ Return unwanted mail. If the mail was sent first class, you can return it to the sender. Do not open the envelope. Instead, write "Refused – return to sender" on the front of the envelope, and put it back in your mailbox for your postal carrier to pick up.

♦ Use their postage to remove yourself from their mailing list. When an organization sends you a request for money, fill out the return form with your name and address, the words (in red!) "Please remove me from your mailing list" written on the form, and "0" written in for the amount. Use the postage-paid envelope to return the form.

♦ Call the toll-free number on the catalog and request that you be removed from the mailing list.

- Write to Mail Preference Service and request that your name be removed from mailing lists. This master list is updated every six months, so you may need to write to them more than once.

  Mail Preference Service
  Direct Marketing Association
  PO Box 9008
  Farmingdale, NY 11735-9008

- To prevent having your credit information released to potential solicitors, call the Credit Reporting Industry Pre-Screening Opt-Out Number at 1-888-567-8688. Choose to opt out forever, not just for two years.

- Sign up for the National Do Not Call Registry. Telemarketers have up to three months to remove your telephone number from their lists, but your number then remains on the list for five years. If you have access to the Internet, you can quickly (and simply) add up to three phone numbers to the list at http://donotcall.gov. No Internet? Call toll-free at 1-888-382-1222 (TTY 1-866-290-4236).

- Take preventative action. Do not return product marketing surveys or registration cards (which are market surveys in disguise), unless doing so is required to activate the warranty. Do not enter sweepstakes. If you order from a company, clearly state that it is not to share your name with anyone else, nor to put you on its mailing list.

- Tell telephone solicitors to put you on their "do not call" list.

Lest you feel guilty for saying *no*, remember that you are doing these businesses a favor. It is a waste of time and money to be marketing to someone who isn't going to buy. You do them a disservice when you let them continue to bark up the wrong tree.

Also, as you practice saying *no* to unwanted sales pitches, remember your manners. Chances are that the person calling you during dinner is just some poor soul trying to make a living. Be nice. Tell them *no, thank you*, ask that they put you on their do-not-call list, then say goodbye. Kindness begets kindness, and it's up to each of us to bring as much as possible into the world.

Close the Door

What about interruptions? It's hard to stay focused when others are constantly asking for our attention. Whether it is our secretary repeatedly buzzing us with questions while we are trying to complete a report, our children wanting us to play with them while we're trying to pay the bills, our computer chirping that "You've got mail!" or our phone ringing while we are making love—it seems someone is always wanting to draw us away from our matter at hand.

Again, we are allowed to say *no*. If we are trying to complete a project, we can set aside "do not disturb" time. For example, we can tell our co-workers (or our children) that we are not to be disturbed for any reason (barring true emergencies, such as the house being on fire) between 9:00 and 11:00 this morning. This only works, however, if we agree to be available at 11:00 to answer any questions that have come up while we were unavailable, and *if we keep our promise*. In order for boundary-setting to work, we must be trustworthy. Other people will not respect our boundaries unless they can trust that we will be available to meet their needs, too.

Technology has made limit-setting easier in some ways. If we don't want to answer the phone—and we don't have to! After all, who's to say that we are home?—answering machines (or voice mail) are quite capable of recording a message. Let the phone ring, and return the call at your convenience.

On the other hand, technology can create boundary-setting challenges. It's tempting to peek at our email each time we're chimed that a new message has arrived. But we are better off resisting the temptation. Instead, check email at regular intervals. Some good times to check are at the beginning of our workday, before lunch, after lunch, mid-afternoon, and once more about a half hour before ending work for the day. Let people know that this is when you check your email, and they will adjust to your schedule.

Pad Your Time

Imagine trying to read this book if the lines ran clear to the end of the page. It'd be hard to do, wouldn't it? Margins create the white space—the boundaries—that make reading possible. Similarly, we need margins in our lives. We call these margins transition time. (I picture transition time as fluffy white clouds, cottony cushions protecting me from crashing headfirst into my next time commitment.) What does it mean to implement transition time? It means padding our calendar to allow for the unforeseeable delay, whether it's a last-minute phone call or a slow-moving logging truck ahead of us. Avoid scheduling events back-to-back. Instead, give yourself some breathing room. We must especially remember to give ourselves time to care for our bodies: a lunch break, a potty break, time to stretch, take a walk around the block, inhale and exhale deeply.

> **"Margin is the gap between rest and exhaustion, the space between breathing freely and suffocating."**
>
> *Dr. Richard Swenson*

Build Fences

One of my favorite boundaries is bender board, a flexible material designed to create borders that my gardener used to build miniature fences around my planting areas. (My garden now has clearly marked vegetable-growing zones, flower-growing zones, and just-hack-it-down zones.) In theory, the bender board is deep enough to discourage unwanted roots from creeping into my flowers and vegetables, thereby reducing the amount of time I need to spend weeding. It also delineates which areas are intentionally planted, providing a clear divider, making it easier to mow and weed-whack. And it supplies a clean line, giving shape and definition to the garden areas.

Use Containers

Perhaps the most commonly used boundary, however, is containers. Usually, I prefer containers that have straight sides (squares, rectangles) because they fit well next to each other, allowing for more efficient use of space. But sometimes round containers are ideal. For example, my gardener reminisced to me about his grandfather's organized collection of hardware—nails, screws, etc. Each category had its own glass jar, the lid of which was permanently fastened onto a horizontal board from which the jars hung. You could see every item easily, and only had to unscrew the jar from its lid to access the hardware of your choice.

Jars are only one type of container. There are so many varieties of vessels from which to choose! (I love going through catalogs and admiring the ingenuity of organizational tools.) Some common containers include:

♦ utensil holders
♦ napkin holders
♦ knife holders
♦ CD, DVD, and cassette holders
♦ bookends
♦ magazine holders
♦ baskets
♦ boxes
♦ buckets
♦ vases, pots, bowls
♦ over-the-seat pocket car organizers
♦ over-the-door pocket jewelry/craft supply/shoe organizers
♦ over-the-door shelving units
♦ accordion pockets
♦ wall pockets
♦ file folders
♦ binders
♦ photo albums
♦ bags
♦ wallets

- purses
- calendars
- appointment books.

Possibilities abound. Storage systems are constructed from every material imaginable. You can find, say, wall pockets made of wood, plastic, wicker, wire mesh, ceramic, canvas, denim…. Imagine it, and it's probably out there, somewhere. No matter what kind of container you choose, though, buy quality. There is nothing more frustrating than a tool that breaks on you.

Resist, however, the temptation to buy a cool-looking container just because it looks like it must be good for something. Refer back to the reality-check questions of Principle #5. Before buying anything, know how you are going to use it and where you will put it.

Dear Claire:

In your workshops, you talk about setting boundaries as one of the 12 organizing principles. But how do you tell someone "no"? I am particularly perplexed by how to handle people who come to my door. I don't want to be rude, so I take their materials, but then I just throw them away. — Marlene

Dear Marlene:

You say "no, thank you" with sincere kindness and a smile on your face. (As Polly Peachum sings in The Threepenny Opera, *when explaining how to maintain a girl's propriety, "Sweetly, but firmly tell him, sorry.")*

People solicit us, for the most part, because they genuinely believe in their cause and the need to spread their word, or because they are trying to raise money, either for their cause or because they need to make a living. Rarely do they knock on our door with the intent of being a nuisance or to do us harm. If we can remember this, remember the person's humanity and sincerity, it is easier to respond to them with kindness.

Granted, solicitors would rather we said yes. Most people do not like to feel rejected. But we don't like to think that someone has said yes when they meant no, that we have been lied to, either.

I spoke with a young man whose religious practice includes going door-to-door to share his faith. He said that he does not want people to take printed information just to get rid of him or to spare hurting his feelings. He prefers an honest "no, thank you." In his view, taking materials that you intend to promptly throw away is a greater rudeness.

Think about this from a business perspective. It costs money to produce marketing materials, whether they be religious pamphlets, flyers promoting a new business, or clothing catalogs. It is a waste of the business' marketing funds to distribute the materials to the wrong market. If you are not interested in the item being offered, say so. It will save the promoters time and money. Saying no *is doing them a favor.*

Ultimately, setting boundaries boils down to a shift in attitude. Too often, we proceed through our lives feeling harried and hurried, put upon by and resentful of others. We demonize solicitors as invaders of our space, set them up as the bad guys. In doing so, we forget our common humanity. We forget the commandment, "Above all, do no harm." We forget how much sweeter the world is when we are gentle with each other, how much happier we are when people are sweet to us.

For several years, I worked with a gentleman who had a kind word for every person—and I mean every person—he spoke with. Whether he was praising the color of your eyes, your clothes, your laughter, your skills, or your personality, his compliments were sincere. Being around him was such a pleasure! He softened people, brought smiles to their eyes.

And that's how we say no: with a smile in our eyes, a kind word for the person who's taking a chance by knocking on our door. (Or calling on the telephone. Remember, telemarketers are people, too—usually people who are just trying to make a living.) Saying yes when we mean no creates resentment and anger. However, every time we are honest—sincerely, with a compliment and compassion—we are making the world a better place. How can that be rude?

7

Dishes before Dusting

Procrastination is the thief of time.

— *Edward Young*

"Dishes before dusting" is an alliterative way to say "prioritize" or "first things first." The problem most people encounter, though, is that they don't know how to decide what comes first. While I might not have an answer to the proverbial dilemma of the chicken vs. the egg, I can help you decide what comes first in most aspects of your life.

The longer we postpone washing dishes, the scarier the kitchen becomes. However, whether we dust weekly or monthly, it takes the same *swoosh* motion to dust. Hence, "dishes before dusting" reminds us to first do the jobs that get worse the longer we put them off.

Other handy rules for prioritizing include: clean from the top, down; clean from dry to wet; work on money in before money out; handle current items before tackling the backlog; and work on things when your energy level is best suited to them. (For me, filing is an end-of-day mindless activity, as is preparing mailings, because I'm shot at the end of the day. Give me mornings for preparing presentations, paying bills, and doing energetic, focused, creative work.)

In her book, *Creating Sacred Space with Feng Shui*, Karen Kingston tells the story about Charles Schwab, who was the president of the Bethlehem Steel Company in the 1930s. He employed a time management consultant, Ivy Lee, to shadow him for two weeks and then advise him on how he could improve his business. The report, when it came, consisted of just three recommendations:

1. Make a list of "Things to Do" every day.
2. Prioritize everything on that list.
3. Tackle things in order of decreasing payoff.

Tools for Determining Payoff

When prioritizing tasks, consider the promises you've made. In general, work on those items that are promised soonest. When juggling promises, examine the consequences of both completing and not completing a task. How important is it? What's the worst that can happen if you don't finish it? If you work on it until finished, how will that affect your ability to deal with other tasks? Which activities are in keeping with your values and goals?

Important vs. Urgent

Stephen Covey, in his book *First Things First*, writes about our culture's addiction to adrenaline and the importance of distinguishing between urgent and important. He has his readers go through a series of values-clarification and goal-setting exercises. Actions that contribute to living our values and achieving our goals are deemed important. Urgent matters are the ones that *others* deem important, and usually are associated with crises and interruptions, with deadlines. Most of us keep ourselves literally cranked up on adrenaline, dousing one fire after another, constantly being hooked in by urgent matters and other people's needs. We become victims, forget why we're here, that we have choice. Covey advises people to distinguish between what is important and what is urgent, and then to schedule in the important activities.

Have to, Want to

Another organizing tool, borrowed from Kathy Waddill's *The Organizing Sourcebook,* is the Require/Desire grid. When we have too much on our plate, we can sort the tasks into the following categories:

Have to/Want to	*Don't Have to/Want to*
Have to/Don't Want to	*Don't Have to/Don't Want to*

Get rid of everything in the bottom right-hand box! After all, if we don't have to *and* we don't want to, what the daylights is it doing on our plate?

Forced Ranking

Sometimes we just don't know what's most important to us. In such a situation, forced ranking is a valuable tool. Forced ranking is a methodical process wherein we list the items we are deciding among, then ask, "Would I rather do this or that, this or that?" on down the list. Make a tally mark next to the preferred activity in each pairing. Once we have compared item one with each following item, we move on to number two and do the same process, then on to number three, and so on until we've completed the list. (For example, would I rather do one or two? One or three? One or four? etc. Then, would I rather do two or three? Two or four? Two or five? etc. Then, three or four? Three or five? Three or six? etc.) When we're done, we rewrite the list in order, from most tally marks on top to least on bottom. If there are any ties—for example, two items with seven tally marks, we ask which of them we'd rather do, then list them as 7a and 7b. The top entries are the ones that are most important to us.

Last, but Really First

Finally, we must take care of ourselves first. Otherwise, there's nothing left of us to take care of others. We need to make sure we get enough sleep, eat properly, drink lots of water, exercise, feed our spirit, and are pampered.

Dear Claire:

I know I'm supposed to handle current tasks first, then tackle backlog items later. But what's current and what's backlog? For example, I have to call a vendor regarding a charge, but first I need to dig through both my husband's and my in-baskets to find the relevant information. I get sidetracked by the piles in the baskets. Also, digging takes time. Shouldn't I handle the in-basket items before calling the vendor? — Barbara

Dear Barbara:

You should organize the in-basket items first, but not process all of them.

At my workshops, I teach 12 basic principles of organizing that I consider crucial. Principle #1 is to think: think verbs; think vertical; think function; think consequences. Principle #2 is to put like with like. Principle #3 is to keep it simple, which includes creating systems to make life easier.

Let's apply these principles to your in-basket. Walk over to your basket. What's the first paper there? A deposit to enter into Quickbooks? Grab a folder, label it To Enter, and place the deposit in this folder. What's the next paper in your basket? A bill to pay? Create another folder, labeled To Pay, and place the bill therein.

Keep going through your in-basket, placing the papers in appropriate folders, labeled by verb. If in doubt, ask yourself, "What has to be done with this? What is the action?" Typical folder categories include To File, To Pay, To Enter, To Call, To Answer, To Read, To Review, To Do. Remember, think verbs. Then put like with like: bills in To Pay, filing in To File, etc.

Sometimes papers relate more to a project than a task. Maybe you're planning a trip to Hawaii, or are buying a car. Maybe your teenager is accumulating college applications, or you have clippings and quotes for relandscaping the garden. For such projects, create clearly labeled folders ("Hawaii," "Buying a Car,") and keep them with the task files.

Now for "think vertical." Remember: File, don't pile. I recommend that you buy a tiered vertical sorter for your desktop and place your folders upright in it. Another option is to hang wall pockets for the folders. Either option allows you easy access and visibility. I also recommend that you avoid the false economy of buying cheap plastic products. While they may save you money in the short run, in the long run you'll find them breaking more quickly than sturdier metal or wood versions, costing you not only more money, but also time and frustration.

Once you've organized your in-basket into task and project folders, you can prioritize your work and access it quickly. You are current. Stay current by going through your in-basket each day, sorting items into their correct folders. Then handle your tasks based on that day's priorities. Above all, do not use your basket for storage. It is for incoming items only, and should be cleared out regularly.

How to prioritize? I suggest handling bookkeeping items first, taking care of money in (invoicing, collections, deposits) before money out (bill paying). You also need to consider time-related items. Is there a meeting or project coming up that needs preparing for? Do you need to make calls to a different time zone, or during specific hours? Do you have other commitments that need honoring?

Do filing last, during quieter times, or when you're feeling like you need a simple task. Designate the last 15 to 20 minutes of each work-day for cleanup. Use this time to clear your desk, to put everything away, and to file. Not only will you have a sense of completion and serenity, you'll make coming to your desk in the morning a simpler, saner, perhaps even enjoyable prospect.

As for calling that vendor... First organize your in-basket. When you find the invoice from the vendor, put a note on it to call about the charge, and file it in the To Call folder. After the question is cleared up, put the invoice in To Pay if it still needs paying, or in To File if the matter is complete.

By organizing your basket into vertical folders labeled by verb or project, routinely sorting the basket's contents into folders, giving yourself enough time to do your work, and cleaning up at the end of each workday, you will have implemented several organizing principles and made it much easier to handle first things first.

8

Slow Down

and

Pay Attention

The trouble with being in the rat race is even

if you win, you're still a rat.

— *Lily Tomlin*

Although each of these twelve principles is important, I think of Principle #8 as the keystone. Slowing down—and paying attention—is fundamental to implementing any organizational system. It is the Zen practice of being organized.

In his delightful *Buddha's Little Instruction Book*, Jack Kornfield has a number of reminders to slow down and pay attention. "Learn to respond, not react." "Take time every day to sit quietly and listen." "As you walk and eat and travel, be where you are. Otherwise you will miss most of your life."

But slowing down bucks our cultural emphasis on speed and productivity. We are urged to multi-task in order to increase efficiency. To some degree, this makes sense. For example, I have a load of laundry going as I write this chapter. Yet often as not, multi-tasking becomes distracting. I can't tell you how many times a day I head toward one task when another catches my eye and pulls me off course. I can be walking into the kitchen to put away the clean dishes when I notice that the cats need more food and water, so I fill up their bowls; but first I decide the bowls could use a washing, and then I wipe down the water that's splashed on the counter, which means my kitchen towel has become wet, so it needs to be put in the laundry hamper, and on the way to the hamper I notice that the cats have left an unwanted gift that needs to be cleaned up....

Richard Carlson, author of *Don't Sweat the Small Stuff... and it's all small stuff* lists entry #62 as "Do One Thing at a Time." He argues that multi-tasking makes it impossible to be in the present moment. He also asserts that being focused in the present moment on just the task at hand increases one's skills, as well as one's efficiency.

Of course, there's the neo-Buddhist saying, "When you eat, eat. When you read, read. And when you read while eating, read while eating." Whatever you are doing, even if it's more than one thing at once, give it your full attention.

Changing Patterns

Years ago, before I was a professional organizer, I worked as a bookkeeper/office manager/personal assistant for a woman I'll call Miriam. She was a busy professional, usually rushing to be on time, running on adrenaline. Upon her request, I organized her office and desk for her. They looked great, and she was happy.

But only Miriam's environment changed; Miriam remained the same. She still entered a room like a whirlwind, unconsciously tossing items onto her desk or workbench. Within days, any sign of my having been there vanished. This was not a fault of the systems I set up (although nowadays, as a professional organizer, I insist upon organizing *with* a client, not for them). It was a result of Miriam's not using the systems I'd put in place. (In all fairness, her husband wasn't much better. Years later, half-jokingly, he sent me a postcard asking if I knew where his missing sock was—I was always finding lost items for the both of them. The answer, of course, was... on his desk!)

The missing ingredient for Miriam (and her husband) was consciousness. If she had taken an extra moment when she entered the room, taken a breath and paid attention, she would have remembered to put things in their places instead of throwing them at the nearest horizontal surface.

Fast-forward eight years to another client whom I'll call Janice. Together we sorted and organized the numerous piles of paper on and surrounding her desk, setting up vertical task files (do, read, answer, pay, enter into computer) in which to process incoming paper. Janice's natural inclination, however, was to make piles, which is how her desk became covered in the first place. In order to avoid recreating the unsightly (to her eyes) mounds of paper, Janice needed to retrain her body—piling was such a deeply ingrained behavior for her. She had to slow down and pay attention to her actions until she built a new habit of storing paper in her files, not piles.

Speed Demons

Like Miriam, we need to stop rushing—particularly when we are driving. Here is a case in point. During a recent summer, the road department was doing a lot of construction on my road, so that we had regular 20- to 30-minute waits. It was a nuisance, and it went on for months, but the locals dealt with it. Except for one guy. One of the flaggers was a very sweet older gentleman whom I'll call John. One day, some guy decided he'd had enough—got mad about having to wait and intentionally hit John with his car, knocked him down to get him out of the way. Thank goodness John was okay, but still... How does that old Talking Heads song go? "Patience is a virtue, but I ain't got the time..."

Another local example comes to mind as testimony to the virtues of slowing down. Because of an inordinate number of fatal auto accidents, the stretch of Highway 101 between Eureka and Arcata was declared a special safety zone, and the speed limit was dropped to 50 mph. Although the speed reduction added maybe a minute to the drive, people invariably complained. But I like the slower speed. This area of California is exquisite, even along the freeways. By driving a bit more slowly, I'm better able to enjoy the scenery: great egrets hunting along the ditches and median strip; light rippling along the tidal waters or, when the tide's out, shimmering off the mud flats; red-shouldered hawks perched along fence posts; dilapidated fences half submerged by flooding tides and rainwater; vivid green pastures dotted with Black Angus and Holsteins; autumnal acrobatic swarms of starlings; rainbows and cloud patterns that never cease to delight.

Indeed, slowing down is part and parcel of Voluntary Simplicity. My writing coach, Zev, chose not to own a car for ten years, largely to simplify his life. By limiting his activities to those he could access by foot or bicycle, he slashed the busyness of multiple errands and resulting hectic schedules to a minimum.

My favorite feng shui consultant, Karen Carrasco, has a gift for seeing our homes as metaphors for our lives. Driving can also be seen as such a metaphor. Driving too fast—hitting the gas pedal, slamming the brake, jerking the steering wheel—stresses a car, causing it to wear down more quickly. It also stresses our bodies, keeping us pumped up on adrenaline, which Cheryl Richardson, author of *Take Time for Your Life*, identifies as the enemy of rest. "The increased speed by which we live has contributed to a society suffering from adrenaline overload... When we use adrenaline as our main source of fuel, our body's adrenal system—the fight or flight response that is supposed to alert us to and prepare us for danger—never has a chance to rest." As I mentioned in Chapter 7, Stephen Covey takes this further. He says we are a culture addicted to adrenaline, that we need to stop jumping to attend the "urgent" (what is important to others) and start serenely attending to our own priorities, to what is "important."

> *The Red Wheelbarrow*
>
> So much depends
>
> upon
>
> a red wheel
>
> barrow
>
> glazed with rain
>
> water
>
> beside the white
>
> chickens.
>
> *William Carlos Williams*

Delight

And then there's Julia Cameron, who wrote *The Artist's Way*. She says this: "My grandmother was gone before I learned the lesson her letters were teaching: survival lies in sanity, and sanity lies in paying attention. Yes, her letters said, Dad's cough is getting worse, we have lost the house, there is no money and no work, but the tiger lilies are blooming, the lizard has found that spot of sun, the roses are holding despite the heat. My grandmother knew what a painful life had taught her: success or failure, the truth of a life really has little to do with its quality. The quality of life is in proportion, always, to the capacity for delight. The capacity for delight is the gift of paying attention."

The Peace of Wild Things

When despair for the world grows in me

and I wake in the night at the least sound

in fear of what my life and my children's lives may be,

I go and lie down where the wood drake

rests in his beauty on the water, and the great heron feeds.

I come into the peace of wild things

who do not tax their lives with forethought

of grief. I come into the presence of still water.

And I feel above me the day-blind stars

waiting with their light. For a time

I rest in the grace of the world, and am free.

Wendell Berry

Dear Claire —

*My life feels frantic and out of control, and my house looks the
way I feel. I'm so busy that I've started misplacing things,
which adds to my stress. I waste precious time looking for lost
items, then wind up being late to appointments. Life is just one
big rush, rush, rush. Help!*   — *Carole*

Dear Carole:

*Sounds like you need to slow down and pay attention. Busyness in itself isn't
your problem; it's a lack of focus.*

*The first thing I recommend is that you slip out of crisis mode. When you
find yourself feeling rushed, confused, or frazzled, stop. Take a deep breath.
Exhale it slowly. Now breathe deeply again. Observe your surroundings and
your situation. Then, calmly choose your next action. Keep returning to your
breath as needed.*

*Conscious deep breathing is the first step. The second is to listen for verbal
cues. Anytime you hear yourself say "I'll just" or "for now," stop. You are
about to defer a decision. (And clutter, my dear, is deferred decisions.)
Breathe. Pay attention. Make a conscious choice.*

*As you focus more on breath, it'll become easier to pay attention to your
actions. Intentionally put items where they belong, rather than letting them
land where they may. (I am assuming you have established homes for things,
and that you simply haven't been putting your toys away. If you don't have a
place for everything, so that everything can be in its place, hire a professional
organizer to help you create appropriate zones and storage within your
home.)*

*Of course, the less you have to put away, the less complicated and messy your
home will feel. So get rid of excess. If an object isn't fundamentally useful
(like a toaster), or doesn't make you smile, what is it doing in your life? Pass
it on to someone who will use it or enjoy it. While you are scaling down your
possessions, work on scaling down your commitments, too. If an activity isn't
nurturing you or taking you closer to your goals, delete it.*

*Finally, carve out time to pamper yourself. Your body needs to remember
what it feels like to relax. So treat yourself to a massage or facial, a hot tub, a
quiet candlelight dinner (cooked, served, and cleaned up by someone else), or
even a nap. Especially if you think you're too busy to do so!*

9

Adopt an Attitude
of Gratitude

*The ultimate prayer, the prayer that comes
from deepest wisdom, is "thank you!"*

— *Sylvia Boorstein*

Much of our clutter comes from hoarding things that we think we might need someday, from keeping things "just in case." This tendency to save everything in preparation for the unknown is particularly common to people who lived through the Great Depression, but is by no means limited to that population. It is a symptom of what is called "scarcity thinking," the belief that there is not enough, that the world is an unsafe place where our needs are not provided for.

And yet, in this very moment, we have everything we need. Right now, in this second, we are okay. Remember the Zen parable about a man and two tigers? Fleeing a tiger, a man caught hold of a vine and swung himself down over the edge of a precipice. Below him, way far below, was a second tiger, eyeing him as a tasty dinner. The man's only safety was that vine. Meanwhile, two mice (one white, one black) started to gnaw at the vine. The man saw a perfect strawberry near him. Grasping the vine with one hand, he picked the strawberry with the other. How sweet it tasted!

Granted, most of us are not Zen masters and are uncomfortable living only in the moment. We need to strike a balance between excessive hoarding and an absolute lack of preparation. After all, even the Fool in the Tarot deck carries a small parcel over his shoulder as he steps off the cliff. So how do we find that balance? How do we free ourselves from scarcity thinking so that we can simplify our lives and let go of those things that we are keeping, not because we love and use them, but because we think we might need them someday?

The trick is to realize that we have enough. The antidote to scarcity is abundance, and the quickest way to abundance is through gratitude. Sarah Ban Breathnach, author of *Simple Abundance: A Daybook of Comfort and Joy*, says it well: "When we do a mental and spiritual inventory of all that we have, we realize that we are very rich indeed. Gratitude gives way to simplicity—the desire to clear out, pare down, and realize the essentials of what we need to truly live well. Simplicity brings with it order, both internally and externally. A sense of order in our life brings us harmony. Harmony provides us with the inner peace we need to appreciate the beauty that surrounds us each day, and beauty opens us to joy." Look at everything we have, at the incredible blessings in our lives!

I, for one, am repeatedly thankful for a roof over my head and indoor plumbing, especially hot running water. I spent three and a half months traveling solo in 1998, mostly tent-camping out of a 1988 Honda Civic. Much of that camping was done in grizzly country, where bear-proofing one's campsite is a must. By the time I ended that trip, I was so happy to have a solid roof to replace the repeated setting up/putting away of my tent. And to have a kitchen with a stove and refrigerator, a sink and cabinets—and no bears! What a luxury it all seemed.

> Be content with what you have;
>
> rejoice in the way things are.
>
> When you realize there is nothing lacking,
>
> the whole world belongs to you.
>
> **Lao Tzu**

Giving Thanks

In addition to her *Daybook*, Sarah Ban Breathnach created a gratitude journal for readers to complete on a daily basis. For those of you who are journal keepers, I recommend it as an inspiring container for writing your daily thanks. I am no longer a journalist, though—writing with pen (or pencil) hurts my hand. So keeping Sarah's gratitude journal didn't work for me. But I like her idea of giving daily thanks, and have adapted it to meet my needs. Every night when I go to bed, after settling under the blankets, I think of at least three things for which I am grateful.

Daily (or nightly) gratitude is exercise for the mind. The same way curls build biceps, giving daily thanks strengthens our "attitude of gratitude." The more we practice thankfulness, the easier it becomes to feel grateful and to see abundance instead of scarcity. Here are a few more activities to build those gratitude muscles.

♦ Say grace. Thank your food—and the cook and farmer and trucker and grocer and baker, everything and everyone who has given of their life energy to bring your sustenance to you—before each meal.

♦ When feeling worried or stressed, name aloud the blessings of your life in that moment.

♦ Compliment others every day. When you notice something that pleases you about someone, tell that person.

♦ Express your gratitude to others. Call, send a card, zip out an email—reach out to others and thank them for the blessings they bring to your world.

Student: Is there anything more miraculous than the wonders of nature?

Master: Yes. Your appreciation of these wonders.

A Poem in Praise

I once attended a Passover Seder where we each named something for which we were grateful. (This activity is more common to Thanksgiving gatherings, but I live in northern California, where we tamper with even the oldest of traditions.) That night, I felt particularly grateful to live in such a beautiful part of the world where I am ceaselessly awed by the grace of the local birds of prey. Inspired, I jotted down the following poem.

Humboldt Hunters: a Prayer of Thanks

A black-shouldered kite

hovers,

white flutter

above green field.

Egrets

hunt along edges, reflected

white,

clear still images

against shallow blue.

Kingfishers perch on phone lines,

red-tailed hawks

in gray snags.

Hens

black and teal,

cluck,

waddle,

and scratch for worms.

It does not matter how we give thanks, be it through journals, poetry, prayer, or some other artistic expression. What matters is that the thanks are given. Gratitude creates the realization of abundance, and abundance heals scarcity. As we move out of scarcity, we shift out of hoarding and into balance. And, as Sarah Ban Breathnach reminds us, we open into serenity and joy.

A Hassidic Tale

One day a very poor man visited a rabbi. The man complained that he had to live in a tiny one-room house with his wife, six children, and mother-in-law. It was so crowded he couldn't stand it any longer; he was losing his mind.

"Do you have any animals?" asked the rabbi.

"Yes, chickens and a goat," the man replied.

"Good," said the rabbi. "Bring the goat into the house to live with you."

The poor man objected, but finally agreed to follow the rabbi's advice. A week later, he came back to the rabbi, even more exasperated. "I brought the goat into my house and now it is worse than before. I can't stand it! What should I do?"

The rabbi instructed, "Go home and bring the chickens into the house to live with you, too." Again the man objected, but finally did as he was told. A week later he came back to the rabbi, dazed and crazed, crying, "It is impossible now in my house, rabbi! Help me!"

The rabbi said, "Go home and take out the goat and the chickens." The man did as he was told and a few days later came back to the rabbi, smiling and grateful. "Rabbi, my house is now so spacious and peaceful! You are certainly the wisest man who ever lived."

> Look at that rainbow.
>
> It is only when the sky cries
>
> that you see the colors
>
> in the light.
>
> T'ao-Shan

10

Base Decisions

in Love

Instead of Fear

Fear is always an anticipation of what has

not yet come.

— Jack Kornfield

What does fear have to do with being organized? Like scarcity thinking, with which it walks hand in hand, fear generates decisions that complicate our lives. Let me give you some examples.

♦ How many of us make extra copies of documents "just in case"? This wastes time and paper, and creates additional clutter.

♦ Before working with me, many of my clients have shaky (at best) paper management systems. Predictably, these people leave out "important" papers because they don't trust that they'll be able to find certain items if they're put away. The result? Multiple and chaotic piles in which "important" paper becomes buried treasure.

♦ Like those extra copies, we purchase multiples of an object in case we lose it or it breaks. This wastes money and adds to our clutter.

♦ Too many of us stay in an unsatisfying job because we believe that we can't do any better. The stress of an unhappy environment can take its toll in a number of ways. Some of us overeat, others overspend, others turn to intoxicants to numb the pain. Study after study show that negative stress is harmful to our health. It also zaps our energy, making it harder to take care of (and organize) our home lives.

♦ And then there are those of us who stay in an abusive relationship because we are afraid to leave. Abuse keeps us in a fight-or-flight cycle, pumped up on adrenaline, which adversely stresses our body. It also disorients our thinking, prompting us to impulsively react instead of sensibly respond. Ultimately, abuse can kill us. If we are being abused, we need to reach out for help.

Love

So what's love got to do with being organized?

If abundance is the antidote to scarcity, then love is the answer to fear. In her book, *Clear Your Clutter with Feng Shui*, Karen Kingston talks about the relationship between love and fear. She writes, "People hold on to their clutter because they are afraid to let it go... However... love and fear cannot exist in the same space, so everything you are holding on to through fear is blocking you [from] having more love in your life... Fear stops you from being who you truly are and doing what you came here to do... [It] suppresses your vital life force energy... Letting go of clutter leaves you free to be you, which is the greatest gift you can ever give yourself."

God

My original wording of this principle was "base decisions in faith instead of fear." But I substituted the word *love* for the word *faith* because, for many people, *faith* conjures

> Simply trust
>
> Do not the petals flutter down,
>
> Just like that?
>
> *Issa*

religious images with which they are uncomfortable. Each of us holds different beliefs about the existence and nature of higher powers. Belief in God is not necessary to implement this principle. For that matter, belief in the goddess isn't necessary, either. What is required is a belief in goodness.

Essentially, basing decisions in love instead of fear means shifting our focus. Instead of anticipating the worst, expect the best. It's the old half-empty, half-full glass. Let's go back to that first example of fear negatively impacting our organizational abilities. The next time we think, "I need two of these! What if I lose one, or it breaks?" consider: What if you don't and it doesn't?

One of my favorite bumper stickers reads, "Encourage your hopes, not your fears." This is the essence of Principle #10. Whether we choose to call it hope or faith or love, it all boils down to the same thing. Like the song says,

> You've gotta accentuate the positive
> Eliminate the negative
> Latch on to the affirmative
> Don't mess with Mister In-Between

If, as Karen Kingston states, love and fear cannot exist in the same space, then holding onto fear prevents love from thriving. Courage is fear that's said its prayers. Let us say ours and make room for love in our lives.

Satori

To live life with an open hand

when fear paints the knuckle

white and anger

closes the fist.

> To remain tender,
>
> pliable when pain hardens
>
> the heart and jealousy
>
> stiffens the neck.

To look at life with eyes wide

open

when grief and sorrow

dim the eye.

> To laugh with a bitter
>
> taste on the tongue
>
> and dance with a stone
>
> in the shoe.

To say yes—

always, yes.

Carla Baku

Dear Claire:

What advice do you have for pack rats? — Andrew

Dear Andrew:

Don't do it.

I know, this is easier said than done for those of you with lifelong, perhaps even inherited, tendencies to squirrel away treasures for those moments when you just might find yourself needing one of the myriad items you've hoarded.

On a practical level, decide what you may reasonably need as regular supplies, be they food staples, eating and cooking utensils, clothing, linens, tools, office supplies, vehicles, or furnishings. Then get rid of the rest, and don't bring any more "treasures" in. Be realistic. Ask yourself, "Do I truly have a current need for this item, a place for it, and the time and energy to deal with it?" (You might benefit from getting someone objective, such as a professional organizer, to help you with this process.)

"But, but..." you protest. No, I'm being firm here. Chances are you have so many items that your space is overcrowded, and you can't find even one pair of scissors among the ten you own, so you wind up being frustrated and possibly even buying an eleventh pair!

Getting rid of the excess (and organizing what's left) helps on a number of levels. It reduces the clutter, which reduces the mess, the dust, and the sense of chaos that leaves one feeling unsettled. It reduces stress because your chances of finding an object improves. It also creates space for new, legitimately useful objects to enter your life. And it saves you money; you no longer buy duplicates or unnecessary items.

On a more spiritual level, hoarding speaks to a lack of faith in the universe to provide for your needs; it stems from what is sometimes called "scarcity thinking." Being organized is ultimately a spiritual practice. You can set up lovely organizing systems, but unless you shift how you move through your world, the systems will be only minimally helpful.

In the case of pack rats, the shift comes in your beliefs. The antidote to scarcity is gratitude, which leads to an awareness of abundance. I strongly suggest a daily gratitude list, spoken or written, whichever works best for you. As you acknowledge daily how much you have to be grateful for, you start to realize just how rich you are, and how perfectly your needs are being provided for. After all, in this moment, you have exactly what you need. The stronger your faith becomes, the more you know how sweet life really is, the more readily you can let go of excess and make room for blessings.

In other words, the more you learn to trust that the universe meets your needs, the more your needs will be met. And the less you will need to be a pack rat, tucking away, "just in case."

11

Remember that

We Have Choices

If your doing doesn't dance with your saying,
you haven't chosen life.

— Reverend Cecil William

Many years ago, I heard a man named Frank suggest that we replace *please* with *thank you* when offering prayers. His point was that everything we need already exists, we have only to acknowledge it. As an example, he proposed this modified Serenity Prayer:

> Thank you for
> the serenity to accept the things I cannot change
> courage to change the things I can
> and the wisdom to know the difference.

The difference, of course, is that we can only change ourselves; we are powerless to change others. Choosing to shift our behaviors and attitudes—which includes accepting others—is one of the most empowering actions we can take.

That Proverbial Rock and a Hard Place

Steve worked as a salesman for a business-supply company. He felt frustrated in his job. Because of his employer's disorganization, there was too much work and not enough time. However, as a fairly new employee, he was in no position to suggest ways to improve the operating systems.

After meditating on the Serenity Prayer, Steve remembered that he could not control his employer, but he could change himself. This insight helped Steve decide where to direct his energy and how to prioritize his time. It also helped him detach from the inefficiencies at work rather than allow them to upset him. And, perhaps most importantly, he realized that he was choosing to work there, that he was not a prisoner of his job. If he wanted, he could look for a different job.

Steve's insight is important. How many of us feel stuck in our jobs, in our lives? And how miserable are we because we feel stuck? And how often do we act out, indulging in self-destructive behavior—using drugs, eating unhealthy food, overspending, neglecting our higher good—to compensate for being miserable?

Too many, too often. But we aren't stuck. We always have a choice. *We may not like our choices, but we still have them.* When we drag ourselves off to a job we hate, we are choosing, for that day, to earn the wages from that job. We enact this choice because we value the things that the money makes possible, be it a humble roof over our heads, food for our children, or a yacht. By remembering that we are choosing to go to our job, we reclaim our power. We walk through that door of our own volition; no longer are we a victim to "I have to" show up. We reclaim our right to direct our own lives—today, in addition to punching the clock at work, we can begin searching for an occupation we love. Choice empowers us to move forward, to take back our life.

An Even Harder Place

Before you dismiss me as an unrealistic Pollyanna, let me admit that there are situations in which choice becomes extremely limited. I am the daughter of a Holocaust survivor. My father lived through the war as a child-in-hiding; both his parents were murdered by the Nazis. The horrors of the death camps are beyond my imagination. But they were too real for many prisoners who could not simply "choose not to go to work that day." Often—if they were so lucky—their choice boiled down, literally, to one of life or death. Which is still a choice, but not one any of us wishes to be forced to make.

Despite the atrocities of the concentration camps, some people maintained their love for humanity and were an inspiration to their fellow prisoners. The reading I've done about the Holocaust all points to the same truth: as Jack Kornfield says, "No one outside ourselves can rule us inwardly. When we know this, we become free." Holocaust survivor Victor Frankl expressed this as "Everything can be taken from a man but...the last of the human freedoms—to choose one's attitude in any given set of circumstances, to choose one's own way."

On a Lighter Note

Choosing our attitude is empowering in our relatively safe and mundane lives, too. For instance, we can find serenity and, consequently, increased efficiency, by shifting how we react to interruptions. A case in point: When I worked as an office manager, I'd feel aggravated if I had to answer the phone while I was focused on writing or bookkeeping. One boss suggested I resolve this irritation by taking a breath and mentally switching hats before picking up the receiver. Taking one extra ring to tell myself, "I am now stopping bill paying and am answering the phone" helped me to stay grounded and greet the caller with a smile in my voice.

> **Claire's ABC's of Organizing**
>
> **Acceptance**
>
> **Being Present (or Breathing)**
>
> **Choice**

Here's another example of the power of choice. Like many of my clients, Molly lives a busy life. She works in the medical field, is enrolled in a master's program at college, serves on the board of directors for a local nonprofit, and is a single mom. Molly also loves to play. She takes several long weekends throughout the year to go skiing or visit her family, and travels to Hawaii at least once a year. Her real passion, though, is quilting. I can't tell you how many times I've shown up for our appointment only to be told, "I've been a bad girl. I quilted all weekend instead of doing my chores."

Molly's favorite chore to avoid, her personal bugaboo, is paper. We usually devote one session each month to processing her mail because she lets it build up, untended. I encourage Molly to recognize that she is choosing to sew or play, and to simply accept the consequences, rather than fear that I'll "bust" her for playing, thereby letting paper get out of control again. Why add to her stress by reprimanding herself? Gradually, as she comes to "own" her choices, she will be able to consciously decide whether or not ignoring the bills in favor of quilting is what she wants at that moment.

To help Molly own her choices, I remind her to watch her language. A few substitutions go a long way. Specifically, instead of saying "I should" or "I have to," say "I can" or "I choose to." "I should call Aunt Mabel" carries a burdensome sense of obligation. "I can call Aunt Mabel" or "I choose to call Aunt Mabel" returns a sense of personal power.

In the Grand Scheme

Every action we take is a choice. Where we live, whom we live with, what we wear, what we eat, what we buy—everything. For years, I had a fading photocopy of the following quote on my refrigerator. I have no idea where it originated, but it serves as an excellent reminder to choose my purchases, and actions, wisely.

> We should see in every disposable fork an oil well up in the Arctic, a pipeline crossing the tundra, a tanker in the straits of Valdez, a refinery creating toxic wastes, a chemical plant polymerizing styrene, a fabricator pressing polystyrene into utensils, and a truck delivering plastic: all that for about 10 minutes of active use.

Julia Butterfly Hill sums this up well. She instructs us to "begin by respecting that all life thrives or dies by our choices. When we truly respect life, rethinking our choices becomes automatic. We discover that we don't need to fill the void with stuff because the greatest things in life aren't things at all and so reducing consumption is easy."

Star Trek's character, Spock, invoked the rabbinical blessing: Live long and prosper. I add to that: Choose well and be happy.

Claire, help!

I've got this box of cards that people have sent to me over the past five years, some of which I haven't even opened. How do I decide what to keep and what to toss? What do I do with the cards I keep? Should I just burn them all? — Ruthie

Dear Ruthie:

The "urge to burn" is common, but don't do it. These boxes are often treasure chests, hiding money and memories in unopened envelopes.

Also, you need to choose what to keep. Otherwise, you're perpetuating the behavior that created the box. The pattern of "I don't know how to deal with this, so I'm going to put it in this box" repeats as "I don't know how to deal with this, so I'm going to burn it."

Organizing is a process of asking (and answering) questions. Start by examining your motives and your resistance by asking, "What would happen if I sorted and processed the contents of this box?"

Next, establish criteria for what to keep. Ask, "Would I regret tossing this if this person were to die tomorrow?" Not everyone and every-thing carry equal importance to us. A card from an acquaintance whom I haven't thought of in years and the yellow sticky from Mom saying, "Here's the article I promised you" can be recycled. (The cards in which she waxed poetic about my virtues, I kept.)

Now ask, "Why am I keeping this and how do I plan to use it?" (And will I realistically use it as intended?) Create homes for the cards according to use. I save them as chronicles of important relationships, so I have file folders for people who are important to me. (Use what-ever works best for you, be it shoe-boxes, manila files, or something else.) Sometimes I save the front of a card to reuse as a postcard. I put this in with my writing supplies. If I were a collage artist, I might store the cards in with art supplies. A painter I know keeps cards in a file labeled "Inspirational Ideas."

Once you've established criteria and created appropriate homes, start sorting. Set aside manageable blocks of time, anywhere from ten to sixty minutes, and stick to that allotment. It's important not to push yourself too hard and to be able to trust yourself; if you say you're working on this task for 15 minutes, then don't exceed 15 minutes. If sorting gets too hard, take a break and schedule a smaller block of time for the next round.

Finally, if you know you won't tackle it on your own, ask for help. Sometimes we need someone to keep us company and help make decisions. I often work with a person to get them started and create a plan that helps them finish the job. They then proceed on their own, calling me with any questions. Their sense of relief and accomplishment when they are done delights them every time.

Good luck with your box. Go slow, have fun, and let me know what treasures you find.

"What we must do is use well the considerable power we have as consumers: the power of choice. We can choose to buy or not to buy, and we can choose what to buy. The standard by which we choose must be the health of the community—and by that we mean the whole community: ourselves, the place where we live, and all the humans and other creatures who live there with us. It is better to buy at a small, privately owned local store than from a chain store. It is better to buy a good product than a bad one. Do not buy anything you don't need. Do everything you can to see that your money stays as long as possible in the local community."

Wendell Berry

12

Ask for Help

It is one of the most beautiful compensations of life that no man can sincerely try to help another, without helping himself.

— John P. Webster

Rugged individualists. Self-made men. Proud. Independent. Pulled up by their own bootstraps. As Americans, we treasure these traits of self-sufficiency. We want to be strong, to complete our work on our own, to (croons Frank Sinatra) "[do] it my way." We avidly wish to avoid being a burden on anybody. Which means the last thing we want to do is ask for help.

And yet we are not isolated beings solely responsible for our own lives and well-being. Rather, we are social creatures, designed to live and work together toward our common—as well as individual—good. None of us can excel at everything. Instead, we each have strengths that we contribute to the whole. One of us bakes, another builds, another creates art, another rears children. By pooling our individual talents, we meet the needs of the entire community.

To some degree, we acknowledge this sharing of responsibilities. We hire experts to handle those tasks that we lack either time, skill, or inclination to do ourselves. We take our car to a mechanic, our taxes to an accountant, our legal problems to an attorney, our health issues to a doctor. There is no shame in hiring a professional for these problems. And yet we resist asking for help from our family, friends, neighbors, or experts, especially for chores—be they housework, schoolwork, errands, or gardening—that we believe we should be able to do ourselves.

I've found that people especially balk at asking for help with getting organized. Many people feel embarrassed, even ashamed, of their chaos and clutter. They believe there is something wrong with them—why can't they do this themselves? Yet being organized is not a moral issue. It is a skill that can be learned.

There is no inherent shame in asking for help. In fact, allowing another to be of assistance can be a gift. Being of service is a *mitzvah*, a blessing. Think of how good you feel when you've done something nice for someone else! When we ask for help (and asking means we are willing to accept the answer *no*), we offer the opportunity for someone to give to us and thereby feel positive within themselves.

Bringing in the Troops

Once we disentangle ourselves from the self-sufficiency trap, asking for help becomes an obvious and welcome solution to our challenges. Here are several examples of bringing in other people to provide assistance and solutions.

Betty is a young widow who, a few years after her husband's death, moved into her own home. With her moved all her deceased husband's belongings, as well as many items that belonged to her now-dead mother. Her garage was packed willy-nilly and wall-to-wall with boxes that needed to be sorted, purged, and organized. It was, to say the least, a daunting task. Upon my suggestion, Betty rounded up a crew of five people, all of whom volunteered to spend a Saturday working with her in exchange for pizza. Working together, the crew unloaded the entire garage, identified contents of the boxes, unpacked the items that lived permanently in the garage (into zones that I'd assigned beforehand), then restacked properly labeled boxes that needed to be sorted for garage sale and give-away into specific, taped-off areas that allowed for quick identification and easy movement around them. In one day, Betty reclaimed her garage, moving it from chaos to clarity.

Darlene suffers from severe back pain from osteoarthritis. Among other restrictions, she can no longer lift heavy items. So how is she to transfer the large bags of dog food from her car into the ant-proof containers in her upstairs apartment? By hiring a neighborhood teen to help. Darlene also is blessed with friends who help her to hang curtains and shampoo rugs.

Gayle rents out the spare room in her house for a reduced rate in exchange for housekeeping services. She and her tenant have a written agreement outlining which chores the tenant is responsible for doing and when. Ida has a similar arrangement, but with a tenant who trades gardening and handyman chores for a reduced rent.

Kirk doesn't mind gardening, but he tends not to do it on his own. So he arranges a trade with his buddy. One weekend they team up to weed Kirk's yard. The next weekend they work together on the friend's garden.

As an administrator, Melinda works a 50- to 60-hour week. She also lives alone. After working long days, Melinda comes home too tired to cook. Yet nutritious food is essential to keeping her body going. So Melinda farms out cooking to someone else's kitchen: her favorite supermarket deli. By buying pre-made healthy meals that require only heating, Melinda keeps herself fed without the extra work of cooking.

Anne, a portrait photographer, originally ran a solo operation. Eventually she brought in her husband as a photographer's assistant, making him responsible for loading all her gear into their van. He was also skilled at engaging the photography subjects, encouraging them to smile and ensuring that their hair was in place and their collars weren't sticking up. As Anne grew in popularity, her business became too busy for the two of them to handle alone. So they hired help, delegating the bookkeeping and office chores to a part-time bookkeeper, and assembly of finished orders to a friend of theirs. They also hired a weekly housekeeper.

Anne's need of paid help is typical of many entrepreneurs. As their ventures grow and thrive, business people find themselves in need of a second pair of hands to handle the administrative angles of business while they tend to the service and product aspects. Secretaries, file clerks, bookkeepers, receptionists, shipping clerks—these supportive positions enable a burgeoning enterprise to burst into full bloom.

Walking My Talk

Lest you suspect that I advocate asking for help while continuing to do everything on my own, let me assure you, I get lots of help in my life! Here is a partial list of tasks that I enlist (or pay) others to do for me:

- gardening
- house painting
- cutting firewood
- building shelves and structures
- plumbing
- preparing tax returns
- repairing and maintaining my car
- healing my cats
- upgrading my computer
- lifting heavy objects
- fetching items from the top shelf at the supermarket
- cleaning up after dinner.

I also rely on others for structure and companionship. For example, I am more likely to stick with an exercise program if I have someone to do it with. Give me a walking buddy with whom I've agreed to walk three times a week, and I'll actually go walking. Left to my own willpower, I'll stay at the computer, writing, or curled up on the couch with a couple of cats and an entertaining novel.

Company also helps me face intimidating tasks. For example, my rider-mower needed a minor repair. I thought I could do it, but I was afraid to try on my own. So I asked a friend to sit with me while I tackled the job. Just knowing that she was coming over motivated me to start repairing it. As it turned out, having her there to lift the mower while I pulled off the tire made the chore much easier, too.

Next to remodeling my home, the biggest project I've ever taken on is writing and publishing this book. Talk about asking others for help! I could not possibly have done this on my own. This book began with friends who nagged me to write and enthused when I confided that I'd begun to organize the material. It grew thanks to my writing coach, Zev, who provided accountability ("I promise to have Chapter 3 done by April 30"), skilled copyediting, and the occasional shoulder to panic on. I knew that Brian, a long-lost friend from 20 years prior (whom I tracked down via the Internet), designs books. Who else would I ask to design this one? Manuscript readers, proofreaders, librarians, printers, distributors...so many people contributed their skills to creating this book you now hold in your hand.

The National Association of Professional Organizers has a motto, "Together we are better." Certainly, together we are stronger. So reach out, ask for help. And offer it. Working together, each of us sharing our gifts, we improve our lives and repair the world; we do the work of *Tikkun Olam*.

Dear Claire:

What's the best way to deal with my business mail? I am flooded with pieces of paper and am tired of spending my days opening envelopes and sorting mail. Please don't tell me to delegate; the nature of my job requires me to see all the mail personally. — Chris

Dear Chris:

It is possible to delegate and still see all the mail, so I am going to tell you to delegate. Have your assistant (I gather you have one, otherwise you would not have mentioned delegating) open the envelopes and, if there is no return address on the enclosed information, attach the envelopes to their contents. (If there is a return address on the item, and if the postmark is not needed, toss the envelopes. They are just more paper you have to deal with later.) Then have your assistant presort for you. This requires you to know your needs and train your assistant to them.

All paper invites one of three possible responses: File, Act, or Toss (F.A.T.). Are you concerned that an assistant would unknowingly toss something you want or file something before you've seen it? Make it clear that you want nothing thrown or filed away, that you will handle this, thank you. And explain why. People work and learn better when they have context for their actions, when they understand how their actions fit into the overall picture.

How should your assistant sort the mail? Put like with like, based on function. What will be done with this item? Is it a bill to pay? An order to fill? A request that needs response? Maybe it's a story idea (if you're a writer or publisher), or a marketing inspiration, or a potential customer. Maybe it's a supply catalog, or an invitation, or a reminder of your dental appointment. Maybe it's vacation information. Or a personal letter from your mother. Whatever. You know what kind of mail you get and how you think of it. Teach these categories to your assistant, at least the broad ones. Your assistant can do an initial sorting of bills, catalogs, periodicals, personal, and other.

You mention "spending your days" dealing with the mail. I suggest you designate a specific time every day for handling the mail. Set aside 15 to 30 minutes (or an hour, if you need) at the same time every day. My personal preference when running offices was to handle the mail right after lunch, but choose the time that works best for you, when you are least likely to be interrupted and when your energy level and attention are matched to the job. Then ask that you not be interrupted for that time period (unless it is an emergency). Treat your mail time as though it were a meeting with an important customer—in a sense, it is! When your staff trusts that you will be available for them afterwards, they will honor your "do not disturb" boundary.

Another time-saver is initially skimming, instead of reading, the mail. We gain a great deal of information from glancing at headlines, bold type, the first sentence of a few paragraphs. Get a quick idea of what the paper is about, then decide why you are keeping it and how you plan to use it. This will tell you where to put it. If it requires action, put it in a task folder (to pay, to enter in computer, to call, information requests to answer, etc.), in a current projects folder (story ideas, marketing ideas, potential customers), or mark it in your calendar and put it in the tickler file (which is where you put all date-related items). If you are saving it for reference, file it according to how you plan to use it. Remember, files are about access, not storage!

Finally, reduce the amount of mail you have to handle by getting yourself off mailing lists. Sort out the unwanted mail as it arrives, then have your assistant (yes, delegate) contact the senders to request that you be removed from their mailing lists. Catalogs have an 800-number for orders; call this number and request that the company remove you from all its lists. Unwanted donation requests often come with a self-addressed envelope. Write "Please remove me from your mailing lists" on the solicitation, stick it in the envelope, and mail it. You can also write to Mail Preference Service (Direct Marketing Association, PO Box 9008, Farmingdale, NY 11735). Include your name and address in all the ways they appear on junk mail that you receive.

The less unwanted mail you receive, the less time you spend handling your mail. Having your assistant open and presort for you, remembering to skim instead of read everything you receive, and setting up a regular time without interruptions will also go a long way toward easing your mail malaise. The easier your tasks, the more productive and efficient you'll be, and the better you'll feel. So let someone help you—by teaching them how. Everyone will be happier for it.

Clutter Clearing Made Easy

In splitting the atom, physicists found that matter and energy are interchangeable, which destroys the categories of both matter and energy. Now the two can't be separated; we are left with matter-energy, a reality held together by the dash. Space-time requires the same dash. Some people write the Almighty's name with a dash: G-D. Maybe the dash in the middle is the key to everything. Maybe it's a minus sign.

— Scoop Nisker

Imagine homes in which rooms are impenetrable because the floors are piled six inches deep with *stuff*, counters are unusable because they are buried under *stuff*, important papers are hidden under other, miscellaneous *stuff*. As a professional organizer, I have seen all of this, and then some. Good consumers that we are, we are consumed in turn by stuff, stuff, and more stuff! But how much of that stuff is of true value to our lives? How much of it makes us happier, healthier, more loved?

Decisions, Decisions

We tend to think of all this stuff as clutter. Actually, *clutter is deferred decisions*. It is everything we haven't decided what to do with, so we leave it out. Even the excess that inundates us is a deferred decision; it is what we've acquired unconsciously, without clear thought and planning.

If clutter is deferred decisions, then getting rid of clutter entails being decisive. Decluttering is a process of asking and answering questions, then acting upon those answers. Of course, knowing which questions to ask helps. Here are some suggestions for clarifying what to keep and what to let go.

♦ To determine which of our belongings are important to us, we can run a what-if scenario. What if I had to move tomorrow; what would I take with me? Or, what if there were a fire; what would I save?

♦ If we are feeling ambivalent, we can assume a decision has been made and ask how we feel. For example, a friend of mine was trying to decide whether or not to buy a house. She had good reasons to buy it, and good reasons not to; the old plus-and-minus list came out about equal. She was torn, not sure what to do. So I prompted her, "Let's pretend that you can't buy the house, that for some reason the sale doesn't go through. How do you feel?" Her answer: "Relieved." Well, then... She quickly decided not to pursue the purchase, and thanked me for helping to clarify her feelings.

♦ When contemplating a particular item, ask, "Why am I keeping this and how do I plan to use it?" ("I don't know" is not an acceptable answer.) By answering this question, we can quickly learn where something belongs. "Because I might be audited by the IRS someday" tells us to file it with our tax records. "Because it'll make a great gift" suggests we keep it with our cache of gifts for others.

In Chapter 5, I mentioned my dear friend, George. Once, when he was organizing his clothing, I saw him put a business card under his t-shirts. Curious, I asked him why he put the card there. He explained that it was a funny card that made him laugh, and he was hiding it under his shirts so that he would be surprised and delighted all over again the next time he found it. Similarly, the client from Chapter 2 who calls her zones "land" stashes little jokes around her kitchen and office that she can find and enjoy anew. For both of these people, the answer to "why am I keeping this?" is "because it makes me laugh." (Is it a coincidence that they both have rubber chickens on display in their homes?)

♦ Do I need to own this, or can I access it elsewhere? For years, I did not own a food processor. I needed one only once a year, to make latkes, and my friends were happy to let me borrow theirs (as long as they could eat their fill of these Hannukah treats). I still prefer to rent all but the most basic tools. And my public library does a much better job of shelving all those books I've read than my little house could do. As for interesting information on, say, feline diabetes, I have no reason to keep paper files because everything I want to know is accessible on the Internet.

♦ How many of these do I need? If we entertain often, then perhaps we have a use for multiple fancy place settings. However, if we habitually eat alone, formal dishes for 12 probably don't get used. Likewise, a family of five uses more sheets, towels, blankets, etc. than does a household of one. And how many sweatshirts does one need? (I know of one compulsive person who collects t-shirts from microbreweries across the U.S. and has them hanging, alphabetically by state, in his closet.)

By applying Principle #5 (Be Realistic), we can create a "Needs List" to use as a guide in getting rid of clutter. For example, assume we decide that we need eight coffee mugs. We then pick our favorite eight mugs and let go of the rest. Whether it's mugs, sheets, or sweatshirts, the list provides structure, a reference to guide us as we navigate what to keep and what to pass on.

♦ Perhaps the most important question is, "Does it make me smile?" If it doesn't make us smile—or isn't genuinely useful—then what is it doing in our life?

> "We are the most materialistic people who have ever lived. We value things over children. Indeed, the way we show how much we value children is by giving them things, to the point where a mother's self-esteem depends on whether she's the first in her neighborhood to get her child some new toy."
>
> *Ramsey Clark, former U.S. Attorney General*

But, But...

Sometimes we resist letting go of an object, even though it isn't serving a useful purpose (which includes bringing us joy). It's important to look at our resistances. Here are the most common ones I've heard.

I might need it someday. Yes, and you might not. This is the same as keeping something "just in case" which, as I discussed in Principle 8, is an example of scarcity thinking. Gratitude teaches us that our needs are being met, and gives us the faith to believe that they will continue to be met. The more we trust life to take care of us, the more life *does* take care of us. So, whenever we hear ourselves say that we're keeping something "just in case," we need to get rid of it. Remember, base decisions in faith instead of fear.

It was a gift (or, it reminds me of someone). The thing is not the person. Keep the gifts and reminders that make us smile, and let go of those that don't. Why taint our relationship with the guilt and bad feelings we experience every time we see the unwanted gift?

Cathy's Closet

Clothes come with their own suitcase of problems. There's an old *Cathy* cartoon in which Cathy is standing in her robe, facing a disheveled, overflowing closet and bemoaning that she has "four outfits I actually wear smashed into three inches of space by six feet of clothes I never wear." She proceeds to explain why she can't get rid of the never-worn objects: because they were too expensive; because they need a few alterations; because they (temporarily, she insists) don't fit; because she never tried hard enough to find something that would match. Let's look at these objections individually.

What good is an expensive gown if it's never worn? Other than for inspiring guilt, that is. Recoup your money, Cathy. Take the gown to a high-class consignment shop, or list it on eBay.

If clothing needs altering, either get it altered or get it out of there. This goes back to Principle #5, Be Realistic. Because I don't sew, I prefer to avoid acquiring anything that needs altering. If you do sew, then make an appointment with yourself to complete the alterations. If, like for me, needles are foreign objects, then implement Principle #12 (Ask for Help) and take the garments to someone who will fix them for you.

How many of us, especially us women, are saving clothes for when we lose enough weight to fit into them again? In general, professional organizers recommend that we get rid of clothes that don't fit, rewarding ourselves with new clothes (which are more likely to be in style) if and when we lose weight. If you cannot bring yourself to donate or sell your "thin" clothes, then at least pack them away. The only clothes that should be in your "getting dressed" zone are the ones you actually wear.

The problem of finding items to match an outfit stops being a problem when we choose our clothes according to our "season." Each of us has a seasonal palette of colors—based on our skin, hair, and eye colors— that looks best on us. Winters and summers radiate in blue-toned colors and either silver or white-gold jewelry; spring and autumn people glow in yellow-toned colors and gold jewelry. Once we've narrowed our clothes to only those colors in our season, we find that everything goes with everything else. We no longer have to search to find the right-colored shirt to go with the odd-colored pants. (For more help in determining your season, read *Color Me Beautiful* by Carole Jackson, or hire a professional color consultant.)

Just Do It

Contrary to common belief and *Cathy* cartoons, the hardest part of clearing clutter is not letting go; it's getting started. Inertia is powerful. Like a ball, clutter at rest tends to stay at rest. However, once we get the decluttering ball moving, we find ourselves on a roll, energized and excited to keep on going.

It's getting that ball rolling in the first place that's difficult. The trick is to start small. Set aside a brief time, 15 to 30 minutes, something manageable. Then declutter a small, clearly defined area—one drawer, or the top of a dresser. The goal is to create a positive experience of success, a sense of accomplishment with a minimum of stress. We want to come away feeling "Hey, I can do this! In fact, I've done it!"

In her book *Organizing from the Inside Out*, Julie Morgenstern introduces the acronym S.P.A.C.E. as a guide to getting rid of clutter. S.P.A.C.E. stands for Sort, Purge, Assign a home, Containerize, and Equalize (keep it put away). This is handy for remembering the sequence when decluttering. In addition, I would like to propose another mnemonic: Claire's C.A.L.M. approach to letting go of clutter.

Choose an area to clear. Touching each item,

Ask—and answer—clarifying questions. (See "Decisions, Decisions.) Implementing Principle #2, put

Like with like within zones based on function. This includes items to donate, to repair, to toss, and to recycle, as well as those you are keeping. Finally,

Maintain your newfound order—pick up regularly, and be conscious about bringing new items into your home.

Tools for Staying C.A.L.M.

Start with clearly labeled containers (paper bags work fine): garbage, recycle, donate/sell, repair, another room, and don't know. Be realistic about the repair category. Only repairs that are simple fixes, such as replacing a battery or sewing on a button, should go into this container. If the chance is low that a significant repair will be done—by you or anyone else—do not put it in the repair container. Also, be wary of the "don't know" category. Remember, clutter is deferred decisions. Every item put in the "don't know" bag is a deferred decision. If you're having trouble deciding, go back to the clarifying questions for guidance.

Some objects are obvious discards. In general, get rid of:

> **Barn's burnt down —**
>
> **Now**
>
> **I can see the moon.**
>
> *Masahide*

- things you no longer use
- things you don't want (including gifts and heirlooms)
- unnecessary duplicates
- things that need fixing that you aren't going to fix
- mystery items
- excess empty boxes, bags, plastic containers, twisties, and recycled envelopes
- big ugly stuff: rusting cars, ratty plants, stuffing-spewing couches.

I Beg to Differ

Please notice that I did not include "Things you haven't used (or worn) in six months." Let me tell you a story to explain why.

Once upon a time, according to Greek mythology, there lived a giant named Procrustes. Procrustes had an iron bed, in which he invited passing travelers to sleep. Hospitable, yes? No. Apparently, Procrustes was a stickler for precision, because his visitors had to fit the bed exactly. If they were too short, they would be stretched to the proper length. If they were too long, their legs would be amputated accordingly. From this story derives the term "Procrustean solution." In essence, a Procrustean solution is one in which a problem is forced to fit an arbitrary answer.

How often have you heard the advice, if you haven't used it in six months (or a year, or any other period of time), get rid of it? Too often, I'm sure. But you will not hear it from me because, to me, this advice is Procrustean. It is arbitrary and externally imposed. I want you to make decisions based on your own needs, values, and goals, not on some magic number dug out of an organizer's advice bag.

Two More Tools

Okay. We know to start with a small, clearly defined area, and to limit ourselves to a manageable amount of time. We know to have sorting bags available and labeled. We know to touch each object, using clarifying questions to decide the fate of that object, then putting it in the appropriate zone or bag. What else do we need to know?

One, we need to implement Principle #12, Ask for Help. However, we want our help to be objective, which usually rules out our family and friends. Instead, I recommend working with a professional organizer who specializes in clearing clutter. Professional organizers encourage clients to stay focused and on task, guide them through making decisions, and contribute a fresh perspective, offering suggestions that clients may not think of on their own. My clients tell me that I provide motivation, structure, humor, compassion, experience, and wisdom, making the process enjoyable and rewarding.

Two, clearing out our clutter is not enough. We need to keep it cleared. Principle #4 teaches us to create habits and schedules. To stay clutter-free, we must build in a routine of daily maintenance, devoting 10 to 15 minutes a day to picking up and purging. We also need to make decisions and take action promptly. Remember, clutter is deferred decisions. Procrastination adds to our problems. Finally, we need to practice setting boundaries and being realistic. Before we say *yes*, we want to check in with ourselves to make sure the *yes* agrees with our values and goals and realistically fits into our life.

Financial Clutter

I am repeatedly amazed by how many people do not balance their checkbooks. Perhaps because I am a bookkeeper, perhaps because I've spent many years living close to the bone—either way, I cannot imagine neglecting to keep my checkbook up-to-date and balanced. And yet I work with client after client who sheepishly confess that they do not keep a running tally of their account balance and have never reconciled their records to the bank's statement.

Financial vagueness is a serious problem for many of my clients, and is part of a pattern of denial and avoidance. To illustrate the pattern, I'll use Joan, a composite of several typical clients, as an example.

Joan's pattern begins with incoming mail, which remains unopened and unsorted. Bills pile up (under junk mail and unread magazines), unpaid. Periodically, in an effort to tidy for impending guests, Joan scoops the piles of mail into boxes or bags, stashed—and then forgotten. Meanwhile, her creditors begin the process of trying to get their money, starting with late fees, progressing to letters of inquiry and threat, and escalating to collection agencies and negative credit ratings. At the same time, Joan is writing checks on an account that may or may not have funds to cover the checks, insisting that she has "an intuitive sense of how much is in there." Unfortunately, her intuition is not psychically connected to the bank's computer, and bounced check fees begin accruing. (One month, Joan was dinged $900 in bank fees!) And then there's her credit card debt from several credit cards, each accumulating higher balances thanks to exorbitant interest rates and late-payment fees.

By the time I meet Joan, she is intimidated by her mail, which represents her financial chaos. To her, incoming mail means angry letters, unmet promises, bills she doesn't know how she'll pay, and a reminder that she is, in her own mind, an inept failure. Her technique for dealing with this mess is to ignore it. Yet her denial no longer works as a coping tool. Rather, it keeps her a victim of the pattern, trapped in her shame and debt.

Jokers and Thieves

Thinking of Joan, I find myself singing the opening lines of Bob Dylan's "All Along the Watchtower"

> There must be some way out of here
> Said the joker to the thief
> There's too much confusion here
> I can't get no relief

There *is* a way out of this mess, not just for Joan, but for all of us who find ourselves having dug similar financial graves. Here are the steps to relief.

1. Open and sort all the mail. Remember that Principle #1 exhorts us to Think Verbs, and that all paper is F.A.T.— file, act, or toss. Sort the mail into task folders, labeled by action—to pay, to call, to answer, to do, to file. Immediately toss all expired offers, outside envelopes (unless you need the address or postmark), propaganda, and inserts into a paper bag for recycling.

2. Keeping the return envelopes with the bills, put the bills in alphabetical order. This is the easiest way to group all invoices from the same place together. Once all the bills are in order, discard the duplicates. You now have an organized pile of only the bills due—a much smaller pile than before you opened and sorted the mail. It's much less intimidating now, isn't it?

3. Assemble your bank statements and check register(s), and balance your register to the most recent bank statement. If you do not know how to do this, either ask a bookkeeper or qualified professional organizer for help, or see if your bank manager can assist you. It is crucial that you identify the accurate amount of money you have in your bank account(s).

4. Create a spending/debt-repayment plan. At this point, it becomes especially helpful to engage the support of others. You may wish to attend a Debtors Anonymous meeting, or make an appointment with Consumer Credit Counseling. Or your bookkeeper, financial advisor, or professional organizer may be able to help you. Jerold Mundis' *How to Get Out of Debt, Stay Out of Debt, and Live Prosperously* goes into detail about the process, but here are a few broad suggestions to get started.

♦ Pay yourself first. Scarcity thinking leads to excess spending. In the same way that the deprivation of dieting pushes us to act out by eating something "bad," the deprivation of a budget, where all our resources go to pay others, prompts us to reward ourselves with purchases we can't honestly afford. Therefore it is imperative that we include something nurturing for ourselves in our spending plan.

♦ Write down every penny spent, including what it was spent on, and every cent earned (or found). This forces us to be conscious of our purchases, much like writing down all our food makes us think before putting something in our mouth. It also helps us see exactly where our money is going, which enables us to make clearer choices about all of our resources.

♦ Set up payment plans to eliminate your debt. One technique is to treat all debtors as equal, dividing the money you have available for debt repayment equitably among all the people to whom you owe money. (It might benefit you to consolidate all your debts so that you only have one debt payment each month.) Another method is called the pyramid technique. This is where you list your debts in order of amount owed, with the least amount on top and the largest on the bottom. Begin by paying off the smallest amount, allocating as much as you can above and beyond the minimum payment each month. Once that debt has been repaid, take the amount you were paying toward it and apply it, plus the minimum you've been paying all along, to the next debt in the pyramid list. One by one, the debts will be paid off. (A variation on the pyramid technique involves paying off the most painful debts first—the one with the highest interest rate, or that's most embarrassing.)

♦ In order to avoid incurring more debt, cancel all but one (some say all) of your credit cards. Label the one credit card "for emergencies only," and do not carry it with you. Instead, pay for purchases with cash, check, or debit card.

5. Maintain the order you've created. Open and sort your mail daily, immediately recycling everything superfluous. Follow through on the items in your task folders—make the phone calls, file the papers, pay the bills, write the letters, and so on. And please, keep your checkbook register balance current, and reconcile it to the bank statement each month when the statement arrives.

Enough Is Enough

In their book Your Money or Your Life: Transforming Your Relationship with Money and Achieving Financial Independence, *Joe Dominguez and Vicki Robin discuss the Fulfillment Curve, which graphs the relationship between feeling fulfilled and the amount of money we spend. Interestingly, there comes a point where our fulfillment drops the more we spend. The peak of the curve—the balanced ideal—is expressed by the concept of having "enough." The goal is to determine how much is enough for yourself, and to let go of the "too much." "So what's all that stuff beyond enough—beyond the peak, where the Fulfillment Curve begins to go down?" the authors ask. "Clutter, that's what! Clutter is anything that is excess—for you.*

"What creates clutter?" they continue. "[M]ost clutter enters our lives through the 'more is better' door. It comes from the disease of materialism, of looking for inner fulfillment in outer possessions. It comes from the early programming that discomfort can be alleviated by something external—a baby bottle, a blanket, a bicycle, a B.A., a BMW or, eventually, another kind of bottle.

"It also comes from unconscious habit. Take gazingus pins. A gazingus pin is any item that you just can't pass by without buying. Everybody has them. They run the gamut from pocket calculators and tiny screwdrivers to pens and chocolate kisses. So there you are in the mall, a shopping robot on your weekly tour of the stations of the crass. You come to the gazingus-pin section and your mind starts cranking out gazingus-pin thoughts: Oh, there's a pink one ... I don't have a pink one ... Oh, that one runs on solar cells ...That would be handy ... My, a waterproof one ... If I don't use it I can always give it away ... Before you know it, an alien arm (attached to your body) has reached out and picked up the gazingus pin, and off you go to the checkout, still functioning like a wind-up zombie. You arrive home with your purchase, put it in the gazingus-pin drawer (along with the five or ten others) and forget about gazingus pins until your next trip to the mall, at which point you come to the gazingus-pin section and ...."

Simplify your life; return to a balanced fulfillment. Ask yourself how much is truly enough. Question whether you truly love and need something before acquiring it. Eliminate the habit of shopping for entertainment. And continue to let go of the excesses that weigh you down. If you haven't already, you'll find that less truly is more.

Conclusion

Those are my principles. If you don't like them, I have others.

— Groucho Marx

In 1998, I created my first "Zen and the Art of Being Organized" class. In 1999, the first newspaper article about me appeared, written by Franci Gallegos (my mother) entitled "The Spiritual Art of Organizing." Also in 1999, I published the first issue of my quarterly newsletter "The Spiritual Art of Being Organized." Six years later, the Spiritual Art has evolved into this book.

Summing It Up

Because it is so inspirational, I often end my workshops by reading Dawn Callan's "Ten Universal Laws of the Warrior Code." It seems fitting, then, to include her Ten Laws at the end of this book, which has been a combination of my newsletters, articles, letters, and workshops.

Ten Universal Laws of the Warrior Code

1. **Pay Attention.** Stay in the present. It's the only place anything is really happening.
2. **Take Responsibility.** This is your life, take it back. Either you get to own it, or you blame someone or something else for it.
3. **No Kvetching.** No whining, no sniveling—it takes you out of the present and lets you abdicate responsibility.
4. **Don't Take Any Shit.** It's very bad for one's self-esteem to take any abuse. Stand up to your tyrants, both internal and external. The cost is too great not to.
5. **Do It Anyway.** Hard choices temper our strength and our integrity; they make the difference between a life of mediocrity and a life of excellence.
6. **Don't Quit.** Look at what stops you, at where you give up the effort. That is the edge between becoming a victim or a warrior.
7. **Keep Your Agreements.** A warrior is only as good as his or her word. The way we build self-trust and trust in others is by making and keeping our agreements.
8. **Keep Your Sense of Humor.** Otherwise, what's the point? Humor helps to stretch beyond ourselves and our own limits.
9. **Love One Another.** Otherwise, where's the meaning? It's the way we remember we're not alone in this universe.
10. **Honor Your Connection to Source.** There is a force in the universe greater than ourselves that creates us, sustains us, provides for us, cares for us, guides us, and loves us. It speaks to us from within. Trust it.

An Alternate Ending

As you've probably noticed by now, my brain throws out snippets of song in response to any number of concepts and situations. (In fact, I was tempted to somehow work *Songs of Freedom* into the title of this book, but decided otherwise.) Here, too, a tuneful lyric runs through my mind. This time the song is from Bertolt Brecht's *The Threepenny Opera*

> Happy endings
> nice and tidy
> it's a rule I
> learned in school
> get your money
> every Friday
> happy endings
> are the rule.

My first year in Humboldt County (before I met my favorite rafting company, Redwoods and Rivers), I wrote the following article. I give it to you here as a happy ending for *The Spiritual Art of Being Organized*.

Going with the Flow

> *I place before you life and death; choose life that*
>
> *ye may live.* — *Deuteronomy 30:19*

I am basking along the bank of New River—river right—just downstream from where a side creek cascades noisily in to join the flow. The sky is blue, the river green, the butterflies a sort of lavender. Perhaps because today is Friday, I have this section of heaven all to myself.

Back home, the sky is gray with coastal overcast. Most people consider today a workday, including me. As a professional organizer, I am blessed with working for myself. And I had planned to work today, but my client called last night to reschedule. My day opened up.

When my client called to say she wasn't ready, a series of choices presented themselves. Should I urge her to keep her appointment with me? Should I worry now that a chunk of income I'd been counting on was suddenly not there? What should I do?

I counsel people to base their decisions in faith, not fear. One aspect of choosing faith over fear is to think in terms of abundance instead of scarcity. This means knowing that there is enough—time, money, love, whatever. It also means staying in the present moment.

I chose to encourage my client to reschedule to a time that worked best for her. I knew without a doubt that, in that moment, I had enough. I may not have had everything I thought I wanted, but I had everything I needed, right then. The money would have helped, but I'd be okay without it. Besides, it didn't disappear; it just happened later. There was no scarcity here.

Which brought me to deciding how I wanted to live today. I ask my clients: What brings you joy? This is where we should focus our energy, because this is where we connect with Source.

What brings me joy? Rivers. Rivers are why I moved here. (Well, rivers and swing dancing—both inspire me to laugh out loud.) But I've been so busy teaching and organizing, which also bring me joy, that I haven't sat beside a river—let alone gone rafting!—since moving here. Until now.

Today, there are no boulders in my river of life. Other days, it seems there are. When an obstacle appears, or when something appears to be an obstacle, I can choose my response. I can choose a path of faith instead of fear, an attitude of abundance instead of scarcity. I can see the rocks ahead as walls, or as surfaces to slide over and around. I can choose to be water dancing with the rocks; I can laugh and gurgle and glide right around them. And so can you.

Acknowledgments

I am delighted to thank all of the following people whose help made this project possible. Thank you to:

My father, Ben Winter, for his precise use of language, his eagle eyes, and his proud encouragement of my efforts. (And for his refusal to let me settle for anything less than right!)

My stepmother, Maridee Winter, for her professional praise, her humor, and her ongoing support.

Karen Carrasco for her enthusiastic belief in me and her beautiful painting of the wild rose for the book's cover.

Rabbi Les Scharnberg for helping track down vital information.

Joyce Johnson, reference librarian at the Eureka branch of the Humboldt County Public Library, for help with navigating the Dewey Decimal system.

Bob Oswell of Macs in the Mist, and my designer, Brian Groppe, for bailing me out when the computer gave me problems.

Catherine Desantis and Louisa Rogers of the Small Business Development Center for their inspired guidance and great company.

Zev Levinson, for being my writing coach. Without him, this book would not exist.

Anthony Raymond, for providing love, roots, and laughter.

My readers, all of whom helped fine-tune this book.

And finally, my clients, for teaching me how

to help them.

Bibliography

Buddha's Little Instruction Book by Jack Kornfield, Bantam Books, 1994; ISBN 0553373854.

Clear Your Clutter with Feng Shui by Karen Kingston, Broadway Books, 1999; ISBN 0767903595.

Color Me Beautiful by Carole Jackson, Ballantine Books, 1985; ISBN 345345886.

Creating Sacred Space with Feng Shui by Karen Kingston, Broadway Books, 1997; ISBN 0553069160.

Don't Sweat the Small Stuff... and it's all small stuff by Richard Carlson, Hyperion, 1997; ISBN 0786881852.

First Things First by Stephen Covey, A. Roger Merrill, and Rebecca R. Merrill, Simon & Schuster, 1994; ISBN 0671864416

How to Get Out of Debt, Stay Out of Debt, and Live Prosperously by Jerrold Mundis, Bantam Books, 1990; ISBN 0553283960.

Organizing from the Inside Out by Julie Morgenstern, Henry Hold and Company, 1998; ISBN 0805056491.

Simple Abundance: A Daybook of Comfort and Joy by Sarah Ban Breathnach, Warner Books, 1995; ISBN 0446519138.

The Artist's Way by Julia Cameron, Jeremy P. Tarcher/Putnam, 1992; ISBN 0874776945.

The Organizing Sourcebook: Nine Strategies for Simplifying Your Life by Kathy Waddill, Contemporary Books, 2001; ISBN 0737304243.

Your Money or Your Life: Transforming Your Relationship with Money and Achieving Financial Independence by Joe Dominguez and Vicki Robin, Penguin Books, 1992; ISBN 0140167153.

Index

About the Author

Claire Josefine is the author of two books: *The Spiritual Art of Being Organized* and *The 12 Basic Principles of Being Organized: 60 Tips Toward a Serene Life.* She has been a professional organizer since 1997, and is a Golden Circle member of the National Association of Professional Organizers.

In addition to writing, Claire conducts workshops and lectures on organizing, and works one-on-one with clients to clear clutter and create organizational systems that make their lives simpler.

As Claire tells it, she began writing *The Spiritual Art of Being Organized* because her friends and clients nagged her to do so. For years, they asked, "When are you going to write a book, Claire?" And then, one day, it was time. She ran into Zev Levinson at a street party and asked him if he'd like to help her write a book. "At first I wanted him to ghostwrite it for me, but as I began to organize my thoughts, I realized that the book had to be in my own voice. (Besides, my English degree had to be put to use somehow!)" And so, with Zev on board for support, she dove in. One year later — on Chinese New Year (year of the monkey) — she finished the manuscript.

Claire's goal for writing this book was to share with others what she'd discovered about organizing, hoping to make their lives easier as a result. "I wanted to collect the wisdom I'd gathered — the poetry, inspirational tidbits, cool quotes, handy tips and, of course, the 12 Basic Principles of Being Organized — into one delightful source."

"I tease my students when I see them taking dutiful notes at the beginning of a class, chiding them 'Where will you put those notes? The kitchen table is not an option!'"

This book takes all those notes, makes them legible, organizes them for easy access, and binds them together into a single book — which can live quite happily on a bookshelf.

About Claire's Cats

Munch – is a tabby and blue-point Siamese cross. My number one big guy, we've been together since his adoption from the free-kitten box in front of a supermarket back in May of 1993.

Ochosi Magdalena – is a little calico and tabby cross. We found her, abandoned, at a campground (site number 8, hence the "ocho" in her name) and lured her into a box with food. She is best friends with Munch, and is my little girl.

Paquito – ah, the blond, blue-eyed, flame-pointed lover boy. Everybody loves Paco. He was my mother's cat, but I knew from the day I met him that someday he'd be mine. When Mom died of lung cancer (a life-long smoker), Paquito joined my household.

Jules – the 12-week old kitten on my shoulder grew up during the course of writing this book. A stocky seal-point, he's delightful, loves to wrassle with Munch and Paquito, and gets along with all the cats.

Sam – was a feral cat (dark gray tabby) who lived on my property before I bought it. The first two years I was here, he avoided me and fought with Munch and Paquito. Then one day he started bounding up to me when I'd whistle for the cats, asking to be petted. Always a sucker for kitty love, I invited him into the house. Now he won't leave my side.

Claire lives with her cats in Northern California, surrounded by dairy pastures, redwoods, and the sounds of the nearby ocean.

Order Form

Yes! Send me more copies of
The Spiritual Art of Being Organized

Telephone orders: 1-800-505-3881

Email orders: organized@humboldt1.com

Postal Orders: Winter's Daughter Press, 7512-A Elk River Road, Eureka, CA 95503, USA.

	# Ordered		Amount Due
1 to 9 books	_____	at $16.95 each	_____
10 or more books	_____	at $12.00 each	_____
		Subtotal	_____

Sales tax: Add 7.25% for books shipped to California addresses _____

Shipping and handling:
U.S.: $4.00 for the first book and $2.00 for each additional book
International: $8.00 for the first book and $4.00 for each additional book _____

Total Amount Due _____

Please make check or money order payable to Claire Josefine

Mail books to:
Name _____
Street Address _____
City, State, Zip _____
email _____